CITY MEMORIES

AN ILLUSTRATED RECORD OF BRADFORD CITY A.F.C.

TRUE NORTH BOOKS

DEAN CLOUGH
HALIFAX
WEST YORKSHIRE
HX3 5AX
TEL 01422 344344

CONTENTS

BRADFORD CITY 1903-1998: THE RECORD
(84 seasons in the Football League)

FA Cup Winners   1911

Promotion	Relegation
From the Second Division 1907/08 Div 2 Champions	**From the First Division** 1921/22
	From the Second Division 1926/27, 1936/37, 1989/90
From the Third Division 1928/29 Div 3(N) Champions 1984/85 Div 3 Champions 1995/96 Div 2 via Play-Offs	**From the Third Division** 1960/61, 1971/72, 1977/78
From the Fourth Division 1968/69 Div 4 4th 1976/77 Div 4 4th 1981/82 Div 4 2nd	**Re-election to the League** 1949 Div 3(N) 1963 Div 4 1966 Div 4

Foreword by David Markham

There is nothing more fascinating to football players and supporters than to look at old pictures of individual players or team photographs. As one grows older the more interesting these photographs become. The photographs also provide a reminder of the passage of time. The young player on the training ground is now a middle aged man. The player scoring a goal 50 years ago is now an old age pensioner.

Bradford City players celebrate winning the Third Division Championship at Bolton on 6th May, 1985. From left to right: Cherry, Jackson, McCall, Abbott, Clegg, Evans, McManus, Withe, Singleton, Campbell and Hendrie.

Trying to name players on team photographs is always a pleasure and a frustration. I don't know about you, but I can usually name three quarters of the squad, but always three or four players, usually those who are on the fringe of the first team or in the reserves elude me.

John Dewhirst and those people who have helped him by lending material deserve the thanks of all City supporters for the wonderful photographs contained in this book and for the memories that will come flooding back when others see them. I am told that there are many equally good photographs that could not be accommodated in the book and that once the book is published John will be stepping up the search for the relatively few team photographs that he has so far failed to track down. Wouldn't it be wonderful if we could have a complete record of all the team photographs covering Bradford City's eventful 95 year history.

The great thing about a book like this is that there is something for everyone. The young supporters will identify with recent photographs, their fathers will look for the photographs of 30 years or more ago and the genuine historians with the various 1911 FA Cup Final shots. All portray not only the personalities but something of the flavour of the time.

We have not been particularly well off for photographs of Bradford City's history and it would be nice to see the pictures in the book and the many others in John's collection put on permanent display. But that is a possible project for the future. For now, I hope that you enjoy this book as much as I have done.

David Markham

Telegraph & Argus, Bradford

First published in Great Britain by True North Books
Dean Clough
Halifax HX3 5AX
1998

© TRUE NORTH BOOKS
ISBN 1 900 463 57 1
City Memories was designed by Mandy Walker, True North Books

Introduction

It has taken three years to collect the photographs and ephemera that have made this book possible. During that time a collection of countless images has been accumulated which record the history of Bradford City and I must acknowledge the assistance of those people who have been prepared to lend items of City memorabilia.

It is not feasible to include a photograph of every player to have made an appearance for the club and indeed the selection that has been compiled is a fraction of what is available. However I believe that what has been included provides a good record of the main events and the key personalities in the club's existence.

What is particularly satisfying is that many of these items have previously been long forgotten or sat in private collections. This publication should at least make them accessible to a wider audience and provide an awareness of Bradford City's history beyond pure statistics.

If there is sufficient demand it may be possible to produce a sequel to CITY MEMORIES and if anyone has interesting items of City memorabilia that could be used I should be grateful if they would contact me through TRUE NORTH BOOKS. For those people interested in the history of the club I would like to mention two recent works by myself and Dave Pendleton of THE CITY GENT. The first, 'Along the Midland Road', provides a history of Valley Parade and is available at the City Shop. The second,

BRADFORD CITY OFFICIAL PROGRAMME.

OFF TO THE PALACE.

NIFFY: "Return Tickets for Crystal Palace, please, for the Bradford City Players——all FIRST-CLASS."

'Paraders Past', is a video featuring the oldest surviving film of Valley Parade from fifty years ago and is on sale at Waterstones, The Wool Exchange price £14.

CITY MEMORIES has been an enjoyable project and I hope that it brings similar enjoyment to the reader (although I apologise in advance if personal heroes have not been included). Bradford City have not had a particularly glamorous or indeed glorious history (notable exceptions apart) but it is fascinating nonetheless. In a contemporary era of million pound signings the photographs included in CITY MEMORIES provide a sobering reminder of the periods of struggle and disappointment in the club's history.

I must thank Dave Pendleton for his excellent research of City personalities in the period preceding the First World War and for his help collecting material. Internet Bantams who have assisted with proof reading should also be acknowledged. Above all I am indebted to my wife, Helen for her patience and support which has been invaluable. The book is dedicated to my children Harry, Sarah and Alison who will have no excuse for not knowing who Bobby Campbell was!

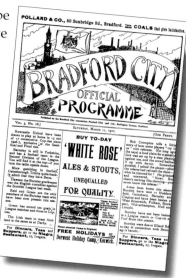

Chapter One
A Golden Age 1903 - 1922

foothold in the rugby stronghold of the woollen region of the West Riding that a Bradford City club was elected to the Second Division of the Football League in May, 1903 without having kicked a ball. The membership of the Manningham club did not get the opportunity to formally consent to the change of codes until four days later at the club's AGM when approval was given by a margin of 75 votes to 34. A period of three months had elapsed between the original proposal for conversion to soccer and the final decision. Thus Bradford City AFC was born. During the summer of 1903 the Manningham management committee recruited players from non-League clubs and others with League experience. With an eye to history, and doubtless the Valley Parade faithful, the new club retained Manningham's claret and amber colours. By contrast Bradford City wore striped shirts as opposed to Manningham's hoops.

Manningham Rugby Football Club was formed in 1880 although the club had been in existence for at least four years as Manningham Albion. In 1886 the Manningham club moved from Carlisle Road to a new ground at Valley Parade. Nine years later Manningham were one of the founder members of the code we know today as Rugby League and won the inaugural championship in 1895/96. The club's main local rival was Bradford RFC (later to become Bradford (Park Avenue) AFC) and this provided the heritage to the intense City-Avenue rivalry of the twentieth century. The competition between the two clubs was also reflected in competition for 'floating' spectators. Following Manningham's relegation at the turn of the century the club's financial position deteriorated significantly and its short term solvency was only secured by the success of an archery competition.

The Manningham officials came to the conclusion that the way to ensure long term survival was through the adoption of the 'round ball' game. So keen were the football authorities to gain a

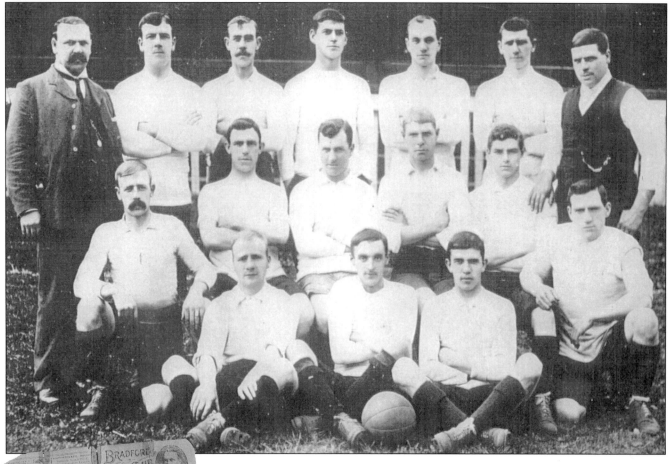

Left and above: City kicked off the first match in their history on 1 September, 1903 at Blundell Park, Grimsby. Perhaps not surprisingly they lost the Second Division match 0-2. The following Saturday on 5 September, City made their first appearance at Valley Parade. Gainsborough Trinity, now a non-League side, were the visitors. The ground was decorated with bunting and flags and the Lord Mayor and Lady Mayoress were in the eleven thousand crowd. Unfortunately the visitors spoiled the party by winning 3-1 but at least the crowd had a City goal to celebrate when, two minutes after the break, Richard Guy scored. According to the Bradford Daily Argus the goal was greeted with 'a shout which awoke babies on the distant hillsides of Bolton and Eccleshill'. City did not have long to wait for their first victory as they won 2-0 at Burton United the following Saturday. The first season was always going to be difficult but City finished a creditable tenth in Division Two.

Bradford City, 1903/04. Left to right, back row: R.Campbell (secretary manager), W. Wilson, S. Bright, A. Seymour, Jas. Halliday, G. Robinson and G. Cutts (trainer). Middle row: R. W. Guy, J. Millar, J. McMillan, T. Farnall, A. Carter and P. O'Rourke. Front row: J. Beckram, J. Forrest and B. Prosser.

Below: George 'Geordie' Robinson's career spanned City's formation and the most successful period of the club's history. Robinson came to Valley Parade from Nottingham Forest in June, 1903 and played in City's first ever match at Grimsby. He captained the side to the Second Division Championship in 1908 and was vice-captain when City won the FA Cup in 1911. The First World War brought an end to his playing career as a right-half as he was already near to retirement. He returned to Valley Parade in 1919 to become City's trainer and held this position until City's relegation from Division One in 1922. Robinson was the only player to play for City in each season prior to World War One and he made 377 League and Cup appearances for City between 1903 and 1915, thereby setting a club record that was not broken for 55 years. Robinson was an ever-present in the team during the 1903/04, 1904/05 and 1909/10 seasons. Although from Nottinghamshire he remained in the city after leaving the club, working in a garage near Valley Parade, and was a regular attender at games. Robinson died in 1945, aged 67.

corner of the ground. This photograph shows the team in August, 1904 in front of the new dressing rooms which were immediately adjacent to the pitch. City improved their League position in 1904/05 by finishing eighth in Division Two. James Conlin (second left, middle row) and James Roberts (third left, back row) represented their respective countries whilst on City's books. Conlin was the first to win his cap when he was selected for England against Scotland in 1906. Although Conlin had been born in England he spent most of his life in Scotland and had been signed from Albion Rovers. He left City at the end of the 1905/06 season to join Manchester City and was later killed at Flanders in 1917. On 7 April, 1906 Roberts won the first of his two Welsh caps whilst at Valley Parade and he remains the only City player to have obtained full international honours for Wales.

Below: Manningham had adopted the Belle Vue Hotel as their headquarters and this was also used as a changing facility by visiting teams. Dressing rooms were not provided at Valley Parade until 1904 when they were constructed at the Bradford end in the south west

Bradford City, 1904/05. From left to right, back row: Holmes (trainer), Forrest, Roberts, Henderson, Mearns, McLean, Robinson, Shinner and R.Campbell (secretary manager). Middle row: Drain, Conlin, Wilson, Graham, McMillan, Farnall, Beckram and Whaites. front: P. O'Rourke and Millar. Inset: Halliday (captain).

Above: Peter O'Rourke was appointed secretary-manager in November, 1905 and was hindered by a number of injuries to key players. In particular O'Rourke had problems with goalkeeping cover and eventually signed the twenty stone Fatty Foulke (left) from Chelsea towards the end of the 1905/06 season. Foulke was the first big-name player to play for Bradford City having previously represented England and appeared in three FA Cup Finals with Sheffield United. O'Rourke experimented with a considerable number of players until he finally assembled the side which won the 1907/08 Second Division Championship. A total of 58 players were selected during the club's first five seasons and a considerable number of those players were Scottish and Irish with very few locals amongst them.

Bradford City, 1906/07. From left to right, back row: P. O'Rourke (secretary), Roberts, Newton, Foulkes, Campbell, Wise, Hanger and Harper (trainer). Middle: Clarke, Millar, Smith, Robinson, Bartlett, Garton, Whaites and Higginson. Front: McLean and Farren.

W. FOULKE.

Below: (both pictures): Frank O'Rourke appeared at Valley Parade in April 1907 playing in a friendly for Airdrieonians. He made such an impression that City officials travelled over to Airdrie's Leeds hotel to rouse him from his bed and sign him. Frank O'Rourke, no relation to Peter, his manager, was an immediate success and became City's record scorer with 93 League and Cup goals - a record broken by Bobby Campbell in 1983. In the FA Cup Final replay of 1911 the press claimed that O'Rourke touched Jimmy Speirs' header before it entered the net but he never claimed the goal and told his friends and family that he didn't touch it. During the First World War he enlisted with the Royal Flying Corps. When his first team career ended in 1915 he became the captain of the reserve side and in 1922 trainer. He retired in June, 1926 and returned to his native Bargeddie in Scotland where he died in 1954, aged 77.

F. O'ROURKE
BRADFORD CITY F.C.

PROMINENT FOOTBALLERS.

Right: A City scout was sent to watch a striker playing for Edinburgh club St.Bernards but it was a different forward who impressed and Jimmy McDonald was signed in April, 1907. At Valley Parade he linked up with George Handley, Wally Smith and Frank O'Rourke and between them they scored 70 goals to play a major part in securing the Second Division championship in 1908. McDonald played in the FA Cup Final of 1911 and captained the side in the days leading up to the First World War. During the war he served in the Royal Field Artillery as a driver. After the war McDonald never really recovered his form and in May, 1920 he left Valley Parade for Raith Rovers although later returned to live in Bradford. McDonald's medals from 1908 and 1911 can be seen above.

J. McDONALD,

BRADFORD CITY.

Above and far left: City won the Second Division Championship with a fairly settled side with players who were reasonably familiar with each other. City were the highest scorers in the entire League with 90 goals but they also had a good defensive record with Robinson, Higginson and Hanger forming an effective combination at the centre of defence. The Scottish international goalkeeper Willie Muir had been signed during the close season although lost his place to Martin Spendiff (top left). Fred Farren played at left back with Robert Campbell at right back. Campbell had been signed the previous season and later played in the 1911 FA Cup Final, making a total of 247 League and Cup appearances for City between 1906 and 1915. City celebrated their championship success with a continental tour in which they played two games, defeating Aix-La-Chappelle 3-0 and Club Sportif Hervietois 6-1.

Bradford City, 1907/08. From left to right, back row: Mr A.Lancaster, Mr I.Newton, Mr C.H.J.Marsden, Mr W.N.Pollack, Mr J.Lucas, Mr J.Nunn and Dr L.Wood. Middle row: C.Harper (trainer), G.Kirk, A.Bartlett, J.Millar, W.Smith, A.Wise, M.Spendiff, S.Higginson, R.Campbell, J.McLean and F.Farren. Front row: T.Sumner, T.McDermott, F.O'Rourke, W.Clarke, G.Robinson (captain), H.Hanger, J.McDonald, G.Handley and Mr P.O'Rourke (secretary).

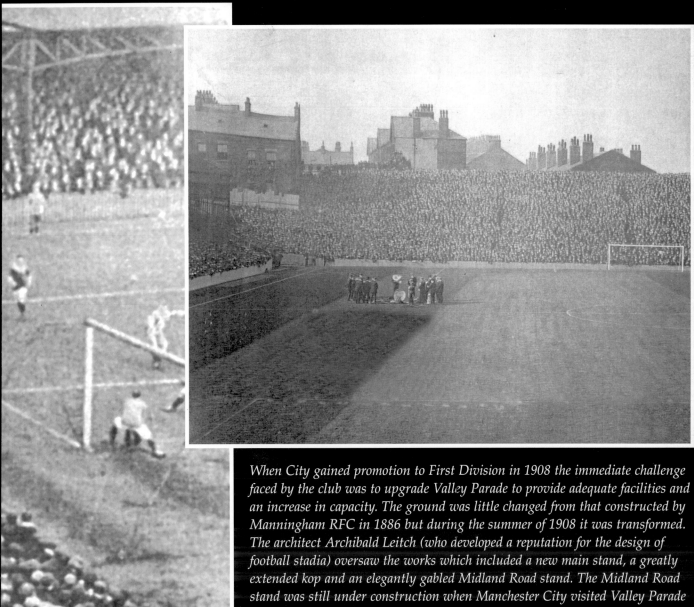

When City gained promotion to First Division in 1908 the immediate challenge faced by the club was to upgrade Valley Parade to provide adequate facilities and an increase in capacity. The ground was little changed from that constructed by Manningham RFC in 1886 but during the summer of 1908 it was transformed. The architect Archibald Leitch (who developed a reputation for the design of football stadia) oversaw the works which included a new main stand, a greatly extended kop and an elegantly gabled Midland Road stand. The Midland Road stand was still under construction when Manchester City visited Valley Parade for City's opening game in Division One. Indeed it wasn't completed until Christmas Day when thirty-six thousand supporters came for the visit of Bristol City. The stadium that was developed remained unaltered until 1952 and was still recognisable in 1985.

Right: The Bradford Daily Argus reported on 8 August, 1908 that 'For the coming season City have adopted a new jersey. All claret body and sleeves, with amber cuffs and a semi-circular amber stripe extending from the shoulder to the centre of the jersey, both back and front. This is surmounted by a badge with suitable device on a woven amber silk background. The new jersey has been designed and supplied by Sports and Pastimes Ltd., football outfitters, 3 Cheapside, Bradford'. The same 'bantams-style' shirt is modelled in this photograph by goalkeeper Mark Mellors who joined City from Sheffield United in March, 1909 for £350. When Mellors arrived at Valley Parade the club was fighting against relegation. He replaced Martin Spendiff and City underwent something of a revival as they fought for their First Division lives. In the penultimate game City lost a two goal lead and dropped a point to Notts County which made relegation appear inevitable. However the defeat in midweek of relegation rivals Manchester City at Bristol City offered a chance of escape provided that City could beat Manchester United at Valley Parade the following evening.

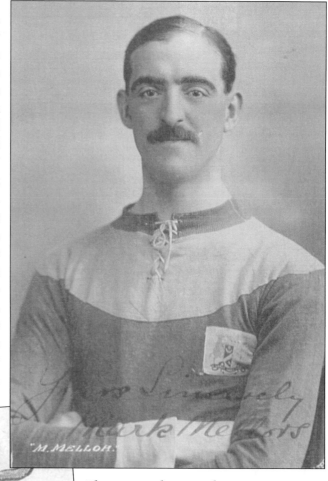

"M. MELLOR."

The atmosphere at that game was extremely tense and even the Manchester City team were present in the thirty thousand crowd. Frank O'Rourke scored his 19th goal of the season in the second half to give City the lead but near the end of the game Mark Mellors was knocked out as he threw himself into the path of a fierce drive. He was literally propped up in the goal as City defended the resulting corner. Determined and frantic defending kept the visitors at bay and City managed to maintain their lead to condemn Manchester City to relegation on the basis of goal average. The supporters ran onto the pitch and Mark Mellors was carried shoulder high from the field. Mellors' greatest feat was yet to come for during the FA Cup winning campaign of 1911 he conceded only one goal. He retired in 1918 and remained in the city becoming a successful wool merchant. He died at his home at Tranmere Park, near Guiseley in 1961, aged 81.

GALLAHER'S CIGARETTES.

E. H. LINTOTT,
BRADFORD CITY, 1909-10.

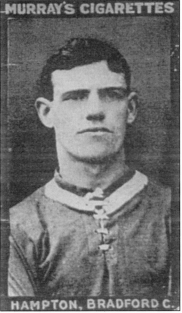

MURRAY'S CIGARETTES

HAMPTON, BRADFORD C.

R. TORRANCE
BRADFORD CITY F.C.

COPE'S "CLIPS" CIGARETTES

No. 152—CHAPLIN
Bradford City
Noted Footballers

Above: This photograph taken in front of the Midland Road stand appeared in the Boys Realm at the end of December, 1909 with the caption: 'Bradford City are a clever First League team and so far have done extremely well this season'. At the time of writing City were very much top of form with eight wins and two draws out of their last ten games. They went into the new year winning five and losing four of their next nine games but finished the season in a creditable seventh position. The team contained three players who won international honours for their country whilst on City's books. Evelyn Lintott (left) had represented the Great Britain team which won the Olympic Gold in 1908 and joined City in November, 1908 from QPR. He played 57 League and Cup games as left-half for City between 1908 and 1912 and won four England caps in 1909. In 1912 he joined Leeds and was later killed on the Somme. Jack Murphy won three caps for Ireland in 1910 and in the same year Dickie Bond represented England three times. Additionally George Chaplin (1910 and 1911), Jimmy Speirs (1910) and later Bob Torrance (1913 and 1914) had trials for Scotland.

Harry Hampton (1910 - 1914) played nine games for Ireland and is City's most capped player.

Bradford City, 1909/10. From left to right, back row: Torrance, Mellors, Campbell and Duffy. Third row: P. O'Rourke (manager), Lintott, Murphy, Chaplin, Henderson, Comrie, McDonald, Speirs, Murray and H. P. Hardman. Second row: Spendiff, Peart, Whittingham, Clark, F. O'Rourke, Handley, Robinson, Logan and Bond. Front row: Grimes, Slemin and Smith.

The winning of the FA Cup in 1911 by Bradford City is surely the highlight of Bradford's sporting history. On 26 April, 1911 Jimmy Speirs' headed goal brought the greatest prize in English sport to Valley Parade. City had fortune on their side from the First Round when Dickie Bond's miskick scored the only goal of the tie with New Brompton (now Gillingham). Norwich and Grimsby were subsequently beaten before Burnley visited Valley Parade in the quarter final. A record crowd of 39,146 saw Frank Thompson (opposite, right) head the winning goal and put City into the semi-finals against the mighty Blackburn Rovers. Few gave City a chance but at Bramall Lane they were 3-0 winners. City's opponents in the Final were Newcastle United and once again City were the underdogs.

Above: Bradford City, FA Cup Finalists 1911. From left to right, back row: P. O'Rourke (secretary manager), Robinson, Campbell, Mellors, Taylor and Harper (trainer). Middle row: Bond, Speirs, F. O'Rourke, Devine and Thompson. Front row: Logan, Gildea and McDonald.

City's eight Scotsmen, two Englishmen (from Nottinghamshire) and one Irishman brought the cup back to the city in which it was designed. At the club's celebration dinner there was loud laughter, along with cheers, when the Lord Mayor of Bradford claimed in his after-dinner speech that the secret of the team's success was Yorkshire grit! The photograph of the team group in front of the Midland Road stand is probably the most revered of all the images that have survived City's 95 year history and subsequent generations of supporters have celebrated 'Glorious 1911'.

Below: The game at Crystal Palace was a disappointment. City's defence held the Newcastle attack at bay and thousands streamed away from the ground before the end as the game petered out to a draw. For the replay at Old Trafford (bottom) City made a surprise change with Bob Torrance replacing William Gildea at centre half. The switch was to be significant and Torrance was widely acclaimed as the 'man of the match'. After fifteen minutes Jimmy Speirs' header slipped past the Newcastle keeper as he was distracted by the incoming Frank O'Rourke (pictured) and City were ahead. The media tried to credit O'Rourke with the goal but the prolific Scotsman admitted that he hadn't touched the ball and so Speirs (to the far right) became the man who won the Cup for City.

Left: Jimmy Speirs is one of City's most famous players, the captain and goalscorer in the FA Cup Final replay and a war hero. Speirs was born in Glasgow in 1886 and began his footballing career in Scotland with Annandale in 1904 before moving onto Maryhill, Glasgow Rangers and Clyde. He joined City in September, 1909. An inside forward, Speirs scored 33 goals in 96 League and Cup appearances. In the 1911 FA Cup Final replay at Old Trafford his headed goal won the Cup for City. Perhaps surprisingly he made only one appearance for Scotland, that being against Wales in 1908. His only other representative game was a Home-Scots v Anglo-Scots trial in 1910. Speirs joined Leeds City in December, 1912 for the then huge fee of £900. When war came he joined the Cameron Highlanders. In a successful military career he attained the rank of sergeant and won the Military Medal. He was killed during the Battle of Passchendaele on 20 August, 1917 and is buried in Dochy Farm New British Cemetery near Ypres, Belgium.

Above: The 1910/11 season was something of a highpoint for Bradford City as they finished 5th in Division One, the highest position they have ever achieved. Back row, left to right: P. O'Rourke (Manager), Chaplin, Spendiff, Bigland, Speirs, Mellors, Lintott, Campbell, Farren, Blair, Maskrey and Robinson. Middle: Torrance, Peart, McDonald, Graham, F. O'Rourke, Young, Logan, Potter and Handley. Front: Menzies (Asst Trainer), Harwood, Dickie Bond, Pimbley, Hampton, Boocock, Anthony Bond, Devine and Harper (Trainer).

Below: City finished the 1911/12 season in eleventh position in Division One but the season was more memorable for the club's defence of the FA Cup. In the Third Round they were drawn away to Second Division neighbours Bradford. The two sides had never met at a senior level but the renewal of the old rivalry captured the popular imagination in the city. A crowd of 24,833 watched the match which was played at a frantic pace. The tie was settled by Frank O'Rourke's goal in the thirteenth minute. Although City progressed to the next round Avenue had proved themselves worthy opponents. It would only be another three seasons before the city of Bradford enjoyed First Division derbies.

Bradford City, 1911/12. Back row from left to right: Graham, Lintott, Thompson.S and Blair. Third row: P. O'Rourke (Manager), Spendiff, Devine, F. O'Rourke., Torrance, Mellors, McDonald, Peart, Cassidy, Hampton, Menzies (Asst Trainer) and Harper (Trainer). Second row: Fox, Gildea, Campbell, Speirs, Robinson, Taylor, Thompson. D and Farren. Front row: Walker, McIlvenny, Logan, Dond, Young and Gane.

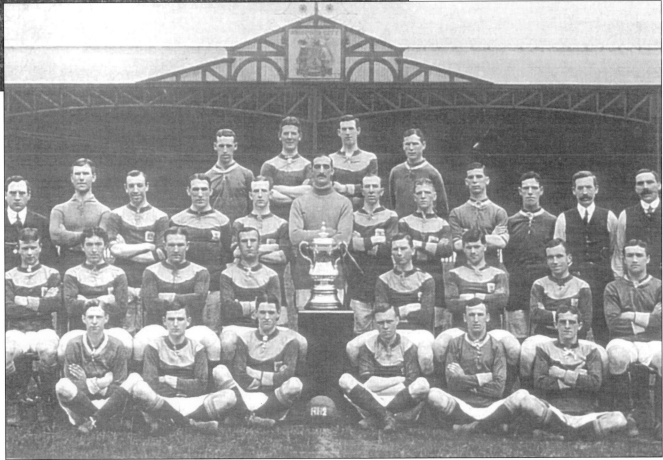

Above: This postcard features the Bradford City team prior to the FA Cup Fourth Round tie at Second Division Barnsley on 9 March, 1912. From left to right (with positions in brackets): Campbell (2), Robinson (4), Boocock (3), Bond (7), Devine (10), Mellors (1), Speirs (8), O'Rourke (9), Logan (11), Torrance (5) and McDonald (6). The first game was drawn 0-0, as was the replay at Valley Parade. A second replay was played at Elland Road which was also goal-less. This meant that City, with Mark Mellors in goal, had conceded only one goal in fourteen Cup ties in 1910/11 and 1911/12 which was a competition record. A third replay was staged at Bramall Lane with a crowd of 38,264 in attendance. Goals from Speirs and Devine (pictured above) gave City a 2-1 lead with a minute to go. Barnsley equalised and then scored a winner in the last minute of extra-time to progress to the next round and ultimately win the FA Cup after a replay.

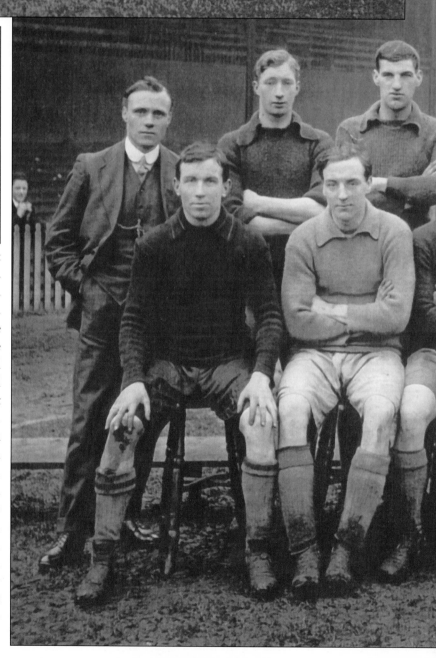

Below: Having finished 5th in 1911 City were unable to consolidate their position near the top of Division One finishing mid-table in the four remaining seasons up to the suspension of League competition in 1915. One of the reasons was that the club could not field a settled team as a result of injuries and the fact that many of the team were coming to the end of their careers and needed replacing. During that period they fielded 60 different players with 36 representing the club in 1911/12 alone. The statistics disguise the fact that there were established regulars in the side such as Dickie Bond, Jimmy McDonald, Peter Logan, Jock Ewart and Bob Torrance. A number of other new players, in particular Irvine Boocock, Jimmy McIlvenny, Oscar Fox, Charlie Storer and later Joe Hargreaves also became regulars. This photograph features the City players in mid-January, 1913 at a time when the team had gone ten games without a win. This was a period of noticeable change for the club with Jimmy Speirs having been sold the previous month and in February Archie Devine was sold to Arsenal with Storer (signed from non-League Gresley) taking his place. Frank O'Rourke returned to the side in January (replacing Harold Walden - a 1912 British Olympic football gold medallist) at centre-forward but was unable to have much impact and Fox ended the season as top scorer with only 13 goals. From left to right, back: Bond, Hargreaves, Gane, Ewart, Wyllie, F.O'Rourke, Campbell and Robinson. Front: Chaplin, Walden, Boocock, P'O'Rourke, Logan, Torrance, Fox and Devine. (Jimmy McDonald, Frank Thompson and Harry Hampton not featured.)

Left: At this time the club's reserve team was successful in the Yorkshire Combination (which hardly provided an adequate level of competition) and latterly in the Central League which it joined in 1912, with the reserves finishing runners-up at the end of their first season. Nevertheless City had to rely upon new signings to strengthen the team although finances prevented the club from acquiring the best players available. Once more the club tended to sign players from Scotland or non-League clubs. In 1914 City invested in two new strikers in the hope of resolving the ongoing problem of a weak forward line in which Frank O'Rourke had been hard to replace. Twenty-nine year old Albert Shepherd arrived from Newcastle United along with Sam Anderson from Hamilton and James Marshall from Partick although their impact was more notable for the support they provided to Oscar Fox who scored 17 League goals in 1914/15.

Right and below:
Avenue and City were First Division rivals for three seasons, either side of World War One. Avenue finished above City in 1914/15 and 1919/20 but then finished bottom in 1920/21 and so were relegated. Of the six First Division derbies City won three and lost once. This programme was for a West Riding County Cup tie in 1913.

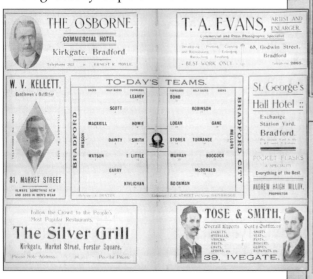

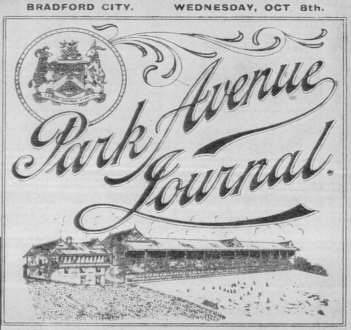

Dated 9 May 191[

Bradford City
FOOTBALL CLUB
(1908) LTD.

Player's Agreement.

Irvine Boocock

Above: One of the few local players to break into the team, Cleckheaton born Irvine Boocock joined the club from local football and made his debut in the First Division against Aston Villa on 5 March, 1910. Although he took time to find his feet, he matured into an outstanding left back and earned recognition by being chosen to represent the Football League on two occasions in 1914. The war arguably prevented him from developing an international career. He enlisted with the Bradford Pals and continued to play for the club whilst on leave. After the war he played for City in the last three seasons in Division One to complete 184 League and Cup appearances. He then spent a season at Darlington before retiring from the game. Boocock was also an accomplished cricketer and appeared for Cleckheaton, East Bierley and Eccleshill in the Bradford League. He even played for a time with Hastings CC. In later years he tended the pitch of Dewsbury and Savile CC. It was whilst cycling home from their ground in 1941 that he lost control of his cycle in Heckmondwike and was killed at the age of 51.

Above and left: In the two seasons before the suspension of League competition Bradford City had a reputation for a very effective defence. In 1913/14 they had the best defensive record in Division One, conceding only 40 goals but equally they scored few goals. That season they scored 40 and the highest scorer was Oscar Fox with nine goals from 33 games. Amazingly nine of the team's 40 goals were scored in three games during November, 1913. The photograph above shows the City team prior to the start of the game with Bolton at Valley Parade on 22 November, 1913. City had

CHURCHMAN'S CIGARETTES.

R. TORRANCE.

won their previous two games beating West Brom at home, 1-0 and Sheffield United away, 3-1. Bolton were defeated 5-1 with the goals scored by Fox (4) and Bond. The team with positions in brackets, from left to right: Campbell (2), Bookman (11), Gane (6), McIlvenny (8), Storer (9), Ewart (1), Robinson (4), Bond (7), Boocock (3), Torrance (5) and Fox (10). In January, 1914 City were the victims of a giant-killing in the FA Cup Second Round by non-League Millwall who beat them 0-1. Later that season Louis Bookman won a cap for Ireland. In the photograph left Jock Ewart is seen in action against Manchester City on 6 April, 1915 at Valley Parade with Irvine Boocock providing support.

Above right: : Robert Torrance was the surprise inclusion in the side that met Newcastle United in the FA Cup replay at Old Trafford, replacing William Gildea at the heart of the defence. His inclusion proved to be a masterstroke for he effectively dealt with the renowned Newcastle attack and was considered to be the man of the match. Born in Kirkintilloch, north west of Glasgow, he joined City from his home town club Kirkintilloch Rob Roy in August, 1908 at the age of 20. The auburn haired Scotsman made his debut against Everton on 28 November, 1908 and was initially deployed at full back but later moved to central defence where he was considered one of the finest players in the land. Torrance made 179 League and Cup appearances for City and played in two Scotland trial games (Anglo-Scots v Home-Scots 1913, 1914). He also made 52 wartime appearances for City, scoring twice and his last game for the club was against Barnsley at Valley Parade on 10 March, 1917. Torrance enlisted as a gunner with 162nd Royal Field Artillery and was killed in action near Ypres, Belgium on 24 April, 1918. Unfortunately he has no known grave and is thus commemorated on the Tyne Cot Memorial to the Missing near Ypres.

Above: By the outbreak of war in 1914 the 1911 FA Cup side had virtually disappeared. Frank O'Rourke, George Robinson and Mark Mellors were all coming to the end of their careers and were not regulars in the team. Jimmy Speirs had been transferred to Second Division Leeds in 1912, Frank Thompson (who had played seven times for Ireland whilst a City player) signed for Clyde in 1913, Archie Devine went to Arsenal in 1913 and Jimmy Blair to Stockport in 1912. Only Bob Torrance, Robert Campbell, James McDonald, Peter Logan and Dickie Bond remained. During the First World War Jimmy Speirs was killed on the Somme in 1916 with former City team mate Evelyn Lintott. Other former players to be killed in action included City's first England international Jimmy Conlin, James Comrie and Gerald Kirk. Bob Torrance was killed in 1917 as were three City reserve players, George Draycott, Ernest Goodwin and Harry Potter. Also injured were Jock Ewart and Frank Buckley. Dickie Bond was captured on the Somme whilst serving with the Bradford Pals and before City played Arsenal in

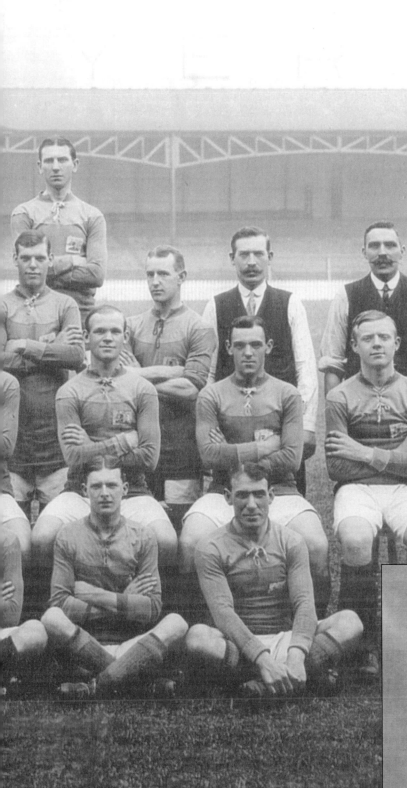

Below: Dickie Bond was a key member of City's side and the first choice no. 7 in his nine seasons with the club from 1909/10 to 1921/22. Bond had been a member of the Preston team that finished second in Division One in 1906 and during his time at Deepdale had been capped for England. He joined City in 1909 at the age of 26 and whilst at Valley Parade won three more caps in 1910. Bond missed the 1911 FA Cup Final in controversial circumstances having been suspended for using 'improper language' with the crowd at Arsenal. Only a year earlier he had been suspended by the club following a night out in Otley during December, 1910 with Jimmy McDonald and Robert Campbell. In 1915 Bond joined the Bradford Pals and before departing for the front made several appeals for volunteers at matches. Bond served as a machine gunner at the Battle of the Somme in 1916 and was taken prisoner. He spent two years as a POW but within days of his release he turned out for the club in a Bradford derby at Valley Parade. Following City's relegation from Division One in 1922 Bond left for his native Lancashire to play for Blackburn Rovers. After a long career he retired to become a publican and died aged 77 at Preston in 1955.

January 1921 he laid a wreath at the cenotaph in Whitehall to honour his fallen comrades.

Bradford City, 1913/14. From left to right, back row: Draycott, Fox, Ewart, Mellors, Adams and Robinson. Third row: P.O'Rourke (Manager), Murray, Neill, Hargreaves, Campbell, Chesser, Tremelling, Torrance, Menzies and Harper (coach). Second row: Bond, Grimshaw, Walden, McIlvenny, Wyllie, Logan, Storer, Boocock and Brown. Front: Bookman, Gane, McDonald, Doolan, Potts and F.O'Rourke.

In 1919/20 City reached the last eight in the FA Cup competition. It was the fourth of five occasions in which the club has managed to progress to the quarter-finals (the most recent being in 1975/76). Although they were favourites to win through to the semi-finals City were beaten 0-2 by Second Division Bristol City in March, 1920. It was subsequently claimed that a pre-match visit to the Fry's chocolate factory had been an inappropriate form of preparation for the game. This photograph was taken on 27 September, 1919 prior to the 1-4 defeat at West Bromwich Albion. From left to right (positions in brackets), back row : Joe Hargreaves (4), Irvine Boocock, Craig Brown (3), Jock Ewart (1), Charlie Storer (5), Robert Potts (2) and Donald Duckett (6). Front row: Peter Logan (7), Oscar Fox (8), James Marshall (9), Alex McGinn (10) and George Handley (11). The faces of a club official and manager Peter O'Rourke (back, right) have been superimposed at a later date. The team was weakened due to injury with Logan deputising for Dickie Bond, Brown for Boocock and McGinn for Jimmy McIlvenny. It is interesting to note that each of the players mentioned had been on the club's books at the time of the outbreak of war in 1914.

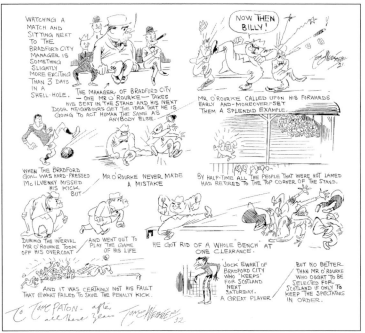

Peacetime football had resumed in August, 1919. The bulk of the City team comprised players who had emerged prior to the suspension of League competition in 1915. They included Jock Ewart, Irvine Boocock, Joe Hargreaves, James McIlvenny, Oscar Fox, James Marshall, Fred Potts, Charlie Storer and Harold Walden. Peter Logan and Jimmy McDonald remained from the 1911 Cup winning team in addition to Dickie Bond. The team was old and past its best but the poor state of the club's finances limited the scope for team strengthening. **Below:** The City squad at the seaside in 1920.

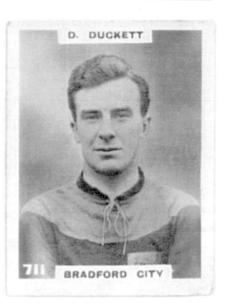

Above: Although new players emerged most of them had limited experience of the First Division. A number were promoted from the reserves such as Thornton born Donald Duckett who became first choice half-back for the next five seasons after making his debut in September, 1919. Duckett formed a defensive partnership with Charlie Storer and Joe Hargreaves before his tragic death in a motorcycle accident in 1924 at the age of 34. Others were signed from junior clubs in Yorkshire, the north and Scotland. William Howson, an inside forward signed from Castleford Town in March, 1920 was one of the few to make any impact. The only signings of note in the first two post-war seasons were Billy Hibbert from Newcastle United in May, 1920 and Arthur Rigby from Crewe in March, 1921. During 1921/22 the club spent an unprecedented £9,000 on new players, most of them from lower leagues with the exception of £3,000 record signing Willie Watson from Aidrie in May, 1921, David Pratt from Celtic in November, 1921 and Andrew Chalmers from Dumbarton in February, 1922. In retrospect the investment in new players came too late but a consequence of the expenditure was that the club was pushed further into debt.

Facing page, bottom: Hibbert's home debut for City at the start of the 1920/21 season was delayed when he broke an ankle bone whilst taking a practice shot at goal prior to the game with Sheffield United. Peter Logan came into the side as the twelfth man (in the days before substitutes were even thought of) and scored a goal in City's 4-0 win. Hibbert missed the next 12 games but finished the season as leading scorer with 13 goals from 29 appearances. Injury prevented Hibbert from playing more than 28 League and Cup games during 1921/22. The fact that he still managed to finish as leading scorer with 15 goals says a lot about the strength of the squad and the team's deficiencies that season.

Bradford City, 1920/21. From left to right, back row: G. Robinson (trainer), F. Potts, J. Hargreaves, J. Ewart, I. Boocock and D. Duckett. Middle row: R. Lindley, O. Fox, W. Hibbert, W. Howson and C. Cook. Front row: R. Bond and P. Logan.

Above and right: During 1921/22 City struggled at the foot of the table for most of the season. In November, 1921 they lost 1-7 at Villa Park where England international Billy Walker scored a hat-trick of penalties against the luckless Paraders. Reserve team player James Barrington had replaced the injured Willie Watson at left back and needless to say he didn't get another chance in the first team. A run of five wins and three draws up to Good Friday appeared to have secured the club's First Division status. With five games of the season remaining a couple more wins would have guaranteed safety. City lost each of those games and in the process were defeated twice by both Birmingham City and Arsenal, fellow strugglers against relegation.

Saturday, March 18th, 1922   SUNDERLAND

BRADFORD CITY A.F.C

PRICE 2ᴰ

OFFICIAL PROGRAMME

Grand Clothing Hall

The Overcoat Specialists
Tyrrel Street & Ivegate Corner, Bradford

Bradford City, 1921/22. from left to right, back row: C. A. Ingram (Financial Secretary), C. Cook, A. Downey, W. Shaw, O. Fox, J. T. Ballantyne and D. L. Menzies (Manager). Third row: L. Busfield (Asst Trainer), C. Kilborn, J. Hay, E. W. Perry, J. Ewart, F. Newton, P. Logan, T. Anderson, R. G. Brown, P. O'Rourke, E. Dixon and G. Robinson (Trainer). Second row: W. Howson, I. Boocock, F. Potts, J. L. Hargreaves, C. Storer, D. Duckett, W. Watson, T. Robb and A. Rigby. Front row: R. Bond, W. Hibbert, J. Barrington and N. J. Winn.

Chapter Two

Decline 1922 - 1937

The recurring theme in the history of Bradford City has been a lack of financial resources and the sale of good players as a significant source of funds. In turn this led to a vicious cycle of weakened teams, poor performances and falling gates with downward pressure on revenue. This was the story during the 1920's and again in the 1930's and it eventually culminated in relegation from Division Two in 1937 and a 48 year exile in the lower divisions.

Above right: Bradford (PA) and Bradford City were each relegated twice during the 1920's and in 1922 both were relegated simultaneously to remain a division apart. Coinciding as it did with the incredible rise of Huddersfield Town (FA Cup winners in 1922 and League Champions in 1924, 1925 and 1926) it was not surprising that public interest in Bradford football declined with significantly lower gates at Park Avenue and Valley Parade. Both clubs had started the decade in the First Division; within five years of the last First Division Bradford derby they were Third Division rivals. *Bradford City, 1924/25. From left to right, back row: Walker, Butler, Bennie, Chalmers and Donaghy. Front row: Watson, Poole, Gallagher, Winn, McLaren and Rigby.*

Below: After relegation from Division One in 1922 City spent five seasons in the bottom third of Division Two, finishing bottom in 1927. During this time the gates averaged between twelve and fourteen thousand, well

below the 22,585 club record average for a season in 1920/21. From 1922, when City were relegated from Division One, until 1927 when they were relegated from Division Two, City lost money in every season except 1924/25 when they reached the last sixteen of the FA Cup. The club managed to survive in this period by making drastic economies and selling its better players such as Dan McKinney who had been selected for Ireland in 1924. In October, 1927 the supporters' club organised a carnival and bazaar to raise funds for the club. Ten thousand copies of the handbook which included a history of Bradford City were sold (facing page).

Bradford City, 1925/26. From left to right, back row: F. O'Rourke (Trainer), P. Bennie, S. Hillier, A. Chalmers, J.S. Poole, J. Smith, G.L. Alcock, P. Logan and C.A. Maley (Asst Trainer). Third row: D.L. Menzies (Secretary Manager), R. Burkinshaw, S. Cheetham, M. Gilhooley, J. McLaren, S. Gallacher, W. Watson, E. Lloyd, W. Shirlaw and L. Busfield (Asst Trainer). Second Row: T. Walker, N.J. Winn, W. Sarvis, R. Foulkes, H. Wright, J. Davis, E. Rees, E. Donaghy and S. McMillan. Front row: J. Fowler, T. Dick and J. Frew.

Left: Harry Wright was signed by the club in September, 1922 from Welbeck Colliery and played 69 times for City as a winger until his release in November, 1927. Wright is seen during a break in training at Valley Parade near the old tunnel (at the corner of the kop and main stand) on 31 July, 1924.

Below: The appointment of Colin Veitch as manager in August 1926 failed to bring the improvement in League standing that had been expected given his fine playing record with Newcastle prior to 1915. City struggled against relegation during the whole of the 1926/27 season and at the half-way stage had won only two out of 21 games. Their last game of the season was away to Manchester City who had been relegated from Division One the previous year and whom City had actually beaten 4-3 five months earlier. Alas City suffered a then record 0-8 defeat at Maine Road in front of a crowd of 49,384 and finished bottom of Division Two.

Bradford City, 1926/27. From left to right, back row:

T. Abraham, S.T. McMillan, S. Gallacher, H. Smith, T.C. Gascoigne and A. Tucker (Trainer). Third row: C.O. Maley (Asst Secretary), A. Cawdry (Asst Trainer), J. Fowler, W. Watson, J. McLaren, W. Shirlaw, H. H. Wallace, W. P. Knox, C. Emmett, C.C.M. Veitch (Secretary Manager) and J. Foster (Asst Manager). Second row: W. Tyler, P. Bennie, W. Hamilton, H. Lovatt, J.S. Poole, M. Gilhooley, G.L. Alcock, E. Lloyd and J.H. Frew. Front row: M. Patterson and G. Ingleden.

BRADFORD CITY A. F. C. SUPPORTERS' CARNIVAL & BAZAAR

OCTOBER 26-29 1927

Below: Frank O'Rourke - Trainer 1922-1926

Presented with "Boys' Magazine"

J. EWART, Bradford City F.C.

Left: One of the big heroes at Valley Parade during the early twenties was Jock Ewart who set a club record for the most goalkeeping appearances in the League that was not beaten until 1995. Ewart had a reputation for making runs upfield although that did not seem to upset his form in goal. He was another player who had joined City from Airdrieonions, in May, 1912 for £1,200, and he made 102 appearances before the outbreak of World War One. Ewart resumed his career with City after the war (having recovered from the shell-shock he suffered whilst serving in the army) before rejoining Airdrie in 1923 for £300 where he helped his club win the Scottish Cup. He returned to Valley Parade for the 1927/28 season when he completed his 283 appearances for the club and then left to join Preston. Ewart represented Scotland in 1921 and kept a clean sheet in a 3-0 defeat of England. Despite the large number of Scots who played for City in the early years he was the only one to obtain full international honours whilst at Valley Parade.

Above: During the summer of 1927 City invested in new players in the hope of achieving promotion but finished their first season in Division Three (North) in sixth position. At the end of that season the club's continuing financial problems came to a head. The players had not received their wages for the last week, the club was in debt and the bank would not extend the overdraft. A restructuring of the board of directors was arranged and funds were pledged from a number of benefactors which allowed the wages to be paid. As an economy measure City resigned from the Central League. It was a reflection of the club's strength in depth and the quality of its playing squad that during the nine seasons in which City competed in the Central League after the war the reserves finished in the bottom three on six occasions, including bottom in 1926 and 1928. Bradford City did not rejoin the Central League until 1982 when the club became a founder member of the second division.

Bradford City, 1927/28. From left to right, back row: E. Lloyd, C. Maley, J. Campbell, J. Foster, C. Veitch, C. Moore, W. Cawdry and D. Ellis. Third row: W. Spence, J. Fowler, A. Bancroft, J. Poole, R. Burkinshaw, J. Morris, S. Barkas, J. Johnson and A. Tucker. Second row: L. Boot, E. Islip, L. Harvey, S. Russell, T. Cairns, W. Watson, A. Scriven, R. Bauld and J. Ewart. Front row: W. Knox and E. Richardson.

Bradford City 4 May, 1929. From left to right, back row: Whitehurst, Cairns, Burkinshaw, Shirlaw, Barkas and Watson. Front row: Russell, Randall, Bauld, Cochrane and Moon.

ROTHERHAM UNITED

2d **Official . .**
Programme

BRADFORD CITY A.F.C.

SEASON 1928-29.

BARRACLOUGH'S

'Edinburgh Castle'
SCOTCH MALT WHISKY
BOTTLE   PINT   HALF-BOTTLE
12/6   9/4   6/6

OLD JAMAICA
RUM
BOTTLE   PINT   HALF-BOTTLE
11/9   8/8   6/2

3/6 per Bottle
FULL RICH
PORT

2/3 per Bottle
TENT
WINE
A PURE FOREIGN WINE

28, IVEGATE, BRADFORD 'Phone 136.

Above and left: The new board appointed Peter O'Rourke as secretary-manager who remains the most successful manager in the club's history having previously been in charge between 1905 and 1921. O'Rourke had also played for City on 43 occasions from the first home game of City's first season in 1903 until November, 1905 when he was promoted to manager. O'Rourke was deeply affected by the death of his son Francis in 1919 and he resigned

Above: The 1928/29 season opened with the record 11-1 defeat of Rotherham United. In February, 1929 City signed Albert Whitehurst from Liverpool who scored 24 goals in only 15 games to the end of the season to set a club record for the most League goals in a whole season. Sadly injury restricted his appearances at Valley Parade and Whitehurst left to join Tranmere in 1931. The 1928/29 season would prove to be the highlight of the inter-war period with gates rising by 50 per cent to an average of 18,551. Bradford (PA) had managed to score 101 goals in each of the three previous seasons in the same division and had been promoted as champions in 1927/28. City emulated Avenue's championship success and when Sam Barkas scored against South Shields at Valley Parade in the last game of the season it set a Third Division record of 128 goals scored. The team conceded only 43 goals that season and benefited from a stable defensive line-up. Goalkeeper Watty Shirlaw was an ever-present that season. At the back of the defence Willie Watson, Sam Russell, Ralph Burkinshaw and William Summers missed only five games between them. Sam Barkas established himself in the team during the second half of the season replacing Bobby Bauld in midfield. In the FA Cup City progressed to the Fourth Round where they were beaten 0-2 at First Division Portsmouth.

as manager in June 1921. He subsequently had brief spells in Wales and Scotland before returning to Bradford to manage Park Avenue. O'Rourke resigned in May 1930 and managed Walsall and Llanelly before retiring in July 1933. He again returned to Bradford and lived next to Valley Parade at 45 Burlington Terrace until his death in 1956, aged 82.

After two seasons in Division Three (North) City returned to the Second Division with high expectations of further progress. In 1929/30 City missed Albert Whitehurst and although replacement centre-forward Alex Cochrane scored 17 goals the team managed to score less than half the number of the previous season. Meanwhile the City defence had one of the worst records in the division. In the event the club avoided relegation by one point and did not secure their status until the last game of the season when they won at Charlton. It is understood that the reason for Peter O'Rourke's resignation as manager in May, 1930 was the refusal of the City board

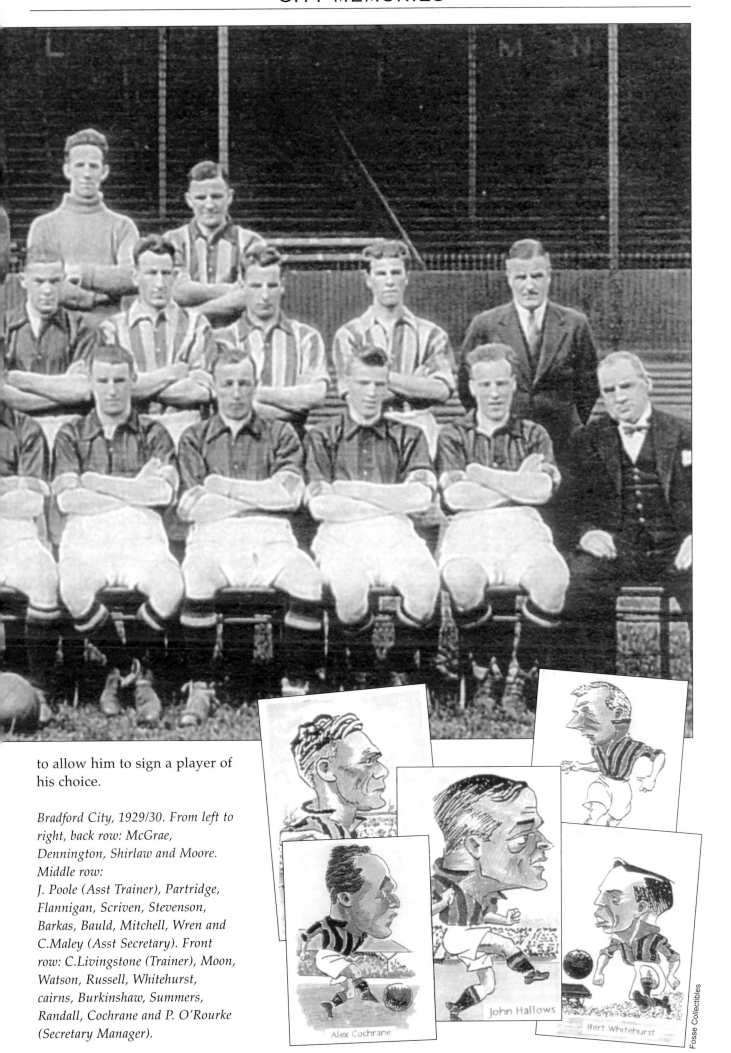

to allow him to sign a player of his choice.

Bradford City, 1929/30. From left to right, back row: McGrae, Dennington, Shirlaw and Moore. Middle row: J. Poole (Asst Trainer), Partridge, Flannigan, Scriven, Stevenson, Barkas, Bauld, Mitchell, Wren and C.Maley (Asst Secretary). Front row: C.Livingstone (Trainer), Moon, Watson, Russell, Whitehurst, cairns, Burkinshaw, Summers, Randall, Cochrane and P. O'Rourke (Secretary Manager).

Alex Cochrane

John Hallows

Bert Whitehurst

Above: This photograph of Bradford City at the start of the 1930/31 season includes a number of the personalities at Valley Parade during the inter-war period. Sam Russell represented Northern Ireland on two occasions whilst on City's books in 1929 and 1930; he was the last current international at Valley Parade before Bobby Campbell played for Northern Ireland in 1982. Tommy Cairns had won seven Championship medals with Rangers before being signed in June, 1927. Cairns did not retire until 1932 at the age of 42 to become the oldest player to have played for the club in a peacetime game. Charlie Moore played 339 League games for City between 1926 and the outbreak of war in 1939. Willie Watson was the club's record £3,000 signing from Airdrie in May, 1921 and played 330 games for City before joining Walsall in August, 1931. Harold Peel had played for Bradford and Arsenal before joining City in 1929 and played a combined 425 games for the two Bradford clubs before retiring in 1936. Full back Charlie Bicknell is pictured as well as his defensive partner Sam Barkas. Albert Whitehurst who scored 24 goals in 19 games during City's 1928/29 Championship season is sat next to trainer, John Poole who had played for the club between 1924 and 1927. Bobby Bauld, Watty Shirlaw and William Summers who were heroes of the 1928/29 season are also in the photograph.

Bradford City, 1930/31. From left to right, back row: W. Watson, J.J. Gill, W. Shirlaw, F. Knox and N. Bruce. Third row: T.E. Robinson (Director), C.A. Maley (Secretary), F.B. Naylor (Director), C. Bicknell, B.A.C. Hall, R. Woolhouse, J. Stevenson, H.B. Peel, R. Bauld, J.R. Gilyard (Vice Chairman), Arthur Smith (Chairman) and J.G. Peart (Manager). Second row: P. Livingston (Trainer), J. Friar, S. Russell, B. Bumford, A. Partridge, A. Peachey, T. Cairns, C. Moore, W. Summers, F. Keetley, S. Barkas, A.J. Whitehurst and J.S. Poole (Asst Trainer). Front row: A. Cochrane, A. Mitchell, W.B. Leeming and A. Scriven.

Below: City established themselves as a mid-table Second Division side during the period 1930 to 1934, finishing as high as sixth place in 1933/34 (a position that was not bettered until 1988). A notable feature of the club's results was the fact that City regularly managed good performances at home which compensated for an unimpressive away record. During the same period however they remained in the shadow of Park Avenue who consistently finished as one of the top sides in the division. City-Avenue derbies attracted particularly high crowds including 34,172 for the game at Valley Parade on 18 January, 1930 (slightly less than the record League gate set on 27 September, 1927 when 37,059 came to see the Bradford derby at Valley Parade). It was claimed that a reluctance by the board to invest in team strengthening in January 1933 when City were top of Division Two cost the club promotion or at least weakened its promotion challenge. This photograph shows the team prior to the start of the 1933/34 season. The first team players are wearing claret and amber shirts with broad stripes and the club crest (Bradford civic coat of arms) which were presented by a local firm in the excitement preceding City's Third Round FA Cup game against Aston Villa at Valley Parade in January, 1933 (the game was drawn and City lost the replay). City continued to wear this style of shirt until 1947 and retained white as the change colour.

Bradford City, 1933/34. From left to right, back row: J. Cliffe, J. Hallows, W. Moore, J. Clarke, K. Haigh, S. Alexander, W. Bruce and J. Collins. Third row: G. Livingstone (Trainer), J. Peart (Manager), J.R. Gilyard (Director), S. Barkas, A. Mitchell, C. Bicknell, S. Warhurst, W. Parker, R. Hamilton, N. James, C. McDermott, T.E. Robinson (Director), C.A. Maley (Secretary), F.B. Naylor (Director) and J. Poole (Asst Trainer). Second row: T.E. Power (Director), J.S. Driver (Chairman), F. Wallbanks, R. Watmough, G. Ebbs, R.Bauld, N. Robson, H. Peel, A. Peachey, C. Moore, J. Roscamp, H. McLaren, W. Burnicle, F. Obank (Director) and A.A. McDermott (Director). Front row: J. Ormandy, J. Horton, J. Spence and T. Barkas.

This page: The fall from grace after relegation in 1922 is reflected in the number of cigarette and collectors' cards that were issued featuring City players. Bradford City had never been a fashionable club and it

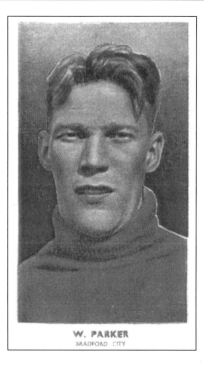

W. PARKER
BRADFORD CITY

CARRERAS CIGARETTES

J. SPENCE
BRADFORD CITY (2ND DIV.)

WILLS'S CIGARETTES

J. HALLOWS (BRADFORD CITY)

was even less so outside Division One. The first national football collectors' cards were produced in Bradford from around 1886 by J. Baines & Co of Oak Lane and later North Parade. Many early Baines cards featured Manningham Football Club, the predecessor of Bradford City FC. City's initial rise to prominence meant that their players began to be featured on cigarette cards and the club is well represented in issues from the period 1907 to 1922. Thereafter there was only a handful of cards featuring Bradford City, a selection of which is featured here. Changes in the tax legislation after the war brought an end to cigarette card issues although football trade cards continued to be published. Needless to say few of those featured City players until the late 1980's.

1932/33

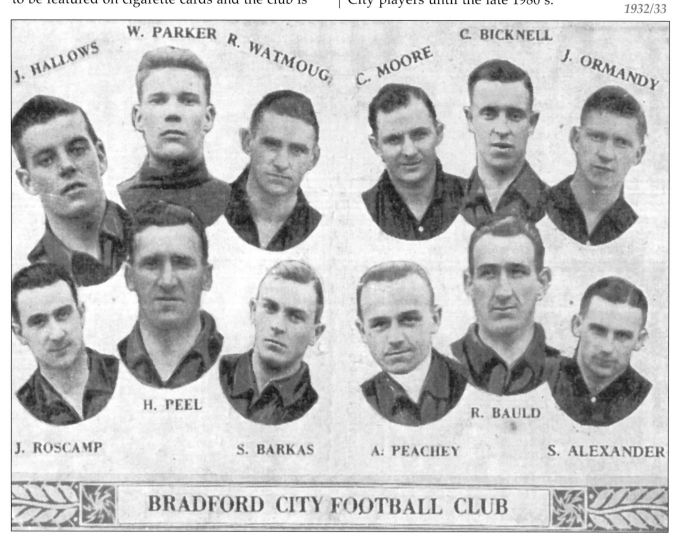

J. HALLOWS   W. PARKER   R. WATMOUG   C. MOORE   C. BICKNELL   J. ORMANDY

H. PEEL   R. BAULD

J. ROSCAMP   S. BARKAS   A. PEACHEY   S. ALEXANDER

BRADFORD CITY FOOTBALL CLUB

BRADFORD CITY

1932/33

Partridge

Gill

Mitchell

Bauld

Barkas

Alexander

Bicknell

Redfern

Watmough

Peel

Ormandy

Fosse Collectibles

Bradford City incurred heavy financial losses in the five years preceding the outbreak of war in 1939 and were forced to sell players to survive. Among the players sold were Sam Barkas to Manchester City in April, 1934; Dick Watmough to Blackpool in October, 1934; Joe Spence to Chesterfield in May, 1935; Charlie Bicknell to West Ham United in March, 1936; John Hallows to Barnsley in March, 1936; George Swindin to Arsenal in April, 1936; Laurie Scott to Arsenal in February, 1937 and then Alf Jeffries and Harry Travis to Derby in February, 1937.

Left back Barkas won First and Second Division Championship medals as Man City captain in 1937 and 1947 and won five England caps (appointed captain in two of those games). Bicknell had made a record 224 consecutive League appearances for City at right back (at the time a League record)

before his transfer to West Ham where he achieved similar standards of consistency. Goalkeeper Swindin had played only 26 League games for City but demonstrated the potential that later benefited Arsenal and which earned him FA Cup and Championship medals. John Hallows had scored a record 74 Division Two goals for City in 164 games since making his debut in the 1930/31 season and is the club's third highest scorer in its history; in January, 1932 he had scored five times in City's 9-1 defeat of Barnsley. Hallows had formed an effective partnership with the former Manchester United and England international Joe Spence during the 1933/34 season. Spence had been leading scorer at Valley Parade with 23 goals in his first season with the club

having been signed by Jack Peart in June, 1933. Full back Laurie Scott made his debut as a teenager in February, 1936 and had made 42 appearances for City by the time of his transfer twelve months later. He won Championship medals with Arsenal in 1938 and 1948 and won an FA Cup medal in the same team as George Swindin in 1950. Scott was also capped by England on 17 occasions between 1947 and 1949. Jeffries and Travis were a couple of young players who had been signed by Dick Ray on free transfers in the 1935 close season. They had both sufficiently impressed against Derby in the FA Cup in February, 1936 that they commanded high fees from the Rams a year later.

Above: Pre-war football programmes bear litttle resemblance to the match day magazines of today. They were designed to provide basic team information, fixture details and brief club news and comment. City's programmes were of particularly poor quality and of a lower standard in terms of design and content than those published at Park Avenue. During the inter-war period City sought to make economies with the costs of printing and this was reflected in the cheap paper used for the programmes. A consequence of this is that Bradford City programmes of the period are quite rare. The City programme was titled 'The Parader' from 1931 until the outbreak of war. During the early years of the club's history newspaper and programme correspondents variously used the identities of 'Paraders', 'Bantams' or 'Citizens' when commenting on Bradford City. (Pre World War One programmes regularly featured cartoons of a bantam and from 1910 there was a sketch featuring a supporter character called Niffy - an early predecessor of The City Gent!) 'Paraders' tended to be used during the inter-war period and after the last war, 'Bantams' was used more frequently as the club nickname. The 'Paraders' identity was revived by Stafford Heginbotham and promoted by the club between 1966 and 1981, falling out of fashion once more to be replaced by 'Bantams'.

Left: Sam Cowan joined City in October, 1935 from Manchester City with whom he had spent 11 years, appearing in three FA Cup Finals, once as a winner in 1934, and winning a Second Division Championship medal in 1928. Cowan had also been capped three times by England. He left City in May, 1937 having played 62 League and Cup games as centre-half.

Above right: : City reached the last sixteen of the FA Cup on three occasions during the period 1922 to 1937, each time as a Second Division club. Memories of FA Cup glory in 1911 were still strong and it was the norm for cup-ties to attract higher than average crowds to Valley Parade. A notable statistic is that

FOOTBALL - C. BICKNELL

between 1911 and 1939 City lost only four FA Cup ties at home out of a total of 30. In 1929/30 City were drawn away at Huddersfield Town in the Fifth Round. Town, the eventual winners of the trophy, won 2-1 in front of 45,659 spectators of which a large number had travelled from Bradford. Other moments of excitement included the defeat of First Division Middlesbrough at Valley Parade during the 1930/31 season and the famous 3-1 giant-killing at Villa Park in 1934/35. In 1935/36 City beat First Division Blackburn at Ewood Park to earn a Fifth Round tie at home to eventual First Division runners-up Derby which attracted a 33,927 crowd. Unfortunately City lost that game 0-1.

The photograph above shows the team that played West Ham at Valley Parade in November, 1934 (a game which City lost 0-2). *From left to right, rear: Keetley (8), Bauld (6), Peachey (5), Warhurst (1), Bicknell (2) and Moore (8). Front: McDermott (3), Hallows (9), Peel (11), Spence (7) and Mitchell (4).* It is assumed that the socks were found prior to kick-off! A couple of players in this team not previously mentioned are Alf Peachey and Charles McDermott who were both popular characters at Valley Parade during the thirties. Peachey left City in September, 1938 having made 201 League and Cup appearances whilst McDermott's career was ended by the war and he formally retired in 1946 at the age of 34.

Below: Bradford City missed relegation by only one place in the 1934/35 season and many City fans blamed this change in fortune upon the sale of Barkas and Watmough. Dick Ray was appointed as manager in April 1935 and in his first full season, 1935/36 City finished a creditable 12th. This was due to impressive home form which included a record eight successive home wins. The following season Avenue and City both struggled at the foot of the division. Avenue finished 1936/37 in 20th position, three points and one place above City who were relegated back into Division Three (North) after winning only once in their last eleven games. Supporters maintained that the squad had continued to be weakened by outgoing transfers and that Ray's replacements had been too late, not to mention of poorer quality. Nonetheless Dick Ray remained a popular manager and most fans were aware of the financial restrictions under which he had to operate. Ray had in fact been relatively successful at recruiting decent players through free transfers or from junior clubs and

maintaining a strong surplus on the transfer account (which is what he was told to achieve).

Bradford City, 1934/35. From left to right, back row: B.Hamilton, G.Pateman, H.Adamson, A.Peachey, J.Horton, J.Clark, C.McDermott, H.Peel, F.Hanson and W.Burnicle. Third row: S.Elliott, T.Fenner, C.Maley (Secretary), J.Peart (Manager), G.Liningstone (Trainer), J.Poole (Asst Trainer), J.Ormandy and T.Barkas. Second row: R.Watmough, C.Bicknell, G.Swindin, S.Warhurst, W.Parker, R.Bauld and F.Wallbanks. Front row: N.James, J.Hallows, A.Mitchell, H.McLaren, W.Bruce, C.Moore, J.Spence and G.Turner.

In April, 1937 both Bradford clubs had LNER steam locomotives named after them. B17 locomotive no.2868 'Bradford City' was the last 'Footballer' class engine to be scrapped in September, 1960.

Right: This photograph features City prior to the 1-5 defeat at Aston Villa in September, 1936. City's goal was scored by George 'Spud' Murphy who played 190 League and Cup games for City between December, 1934 and November, 1947 (not to mention numerous other wartime games).

From left to right, back row: Charlie Moore, John Mackie, Laurie Scott, Sam Warhurst, Harry Sherwin (trainer), Charles McDermott, William Burnicle and Alf Peachey. Front: Alf Jeffries, Walter Bruce, David James, Dick Ray (manager), George Murphy, Roland Bartholomew and Sam Cowan.

play at a new 'continental-style' stadium, possibly at Odsal (which had opened in 1934) with rugby and football staged on alternate Saturdays. The City directors finally rejected the idea in October, 1938 confident that their club could improve its commercial position without the need for merger. The City directors claimed that their club's debts could be cleared with a single transfer, reflecting perhaps the unambitious 'selling mentality' in the boardroom. A lack of finance and a policy of selling good players were primary reasons for the club's relegation in 1937.

However a lack of vision was also a contributory factor in the demise of Bradford City. The outbreak of war in 1939 effectively destroyed the club's chances of rebuilding and making a quick return to Division Two and indeed City were exiled in the lower divisions for the next 48 years.

Above and right: In December 1937 there was an approach from the Bradford (PA) chairman to explore the possibility of the two Bradford clubs amalgamating. It was suggested that the merged club would

Chapter Three

No Escape 1937 - 1958

Bradford City finished their first season back in Division Three (North) in 1937/38 in 14th position with average gates of only six thousand. The following season (1938/39), under the guidance of Fred Westgarth, City finished in third position and there was genuine hope during the summer of 1939 that City could make a realistic promotion challenge. One player who had emerged as a lethal goalscorer during this time was Jack Deakin who was leading scorer in the 1937/38 and 1938/39 seasons when he achieved an impressive scoring rate of 49 goals in 64 League and Cup games. Deakin was only 27 years old when war broke out but by the time it ended it was too late for him to resume his career.

Below: The 1939/40 season was just three games old when war was declared on 3 September and City were in 21st position with only one point. George Hinsley scored City's last pre-war goal and by chance would score their first post-war goal. The Football League was suspended to be replaced by a regional competition. With many regular players unavailable due to wartime service a guest player system was introduced. City did not have the advantage of being close to a garrison but were able to field a number of internationals at various times including Sam Bartram (Charlton), Eric Stephenson (Leeds), Willie Waddell (Rangers) and Andie Beattie (Preston). There was also the incredible instance of Len Shackleton

playing for both City and Avenue on Christmas Day, 1940. Attendances rarely exceeded three thousand although there were a couple of five figure gates for Bradford derbies. Like Park Avenue, Valley Parade was requisitioned by the military and in 1944 the ground was only available to the club for first team fixtures on Saturdays.

Below right: July, 1943 brought the shock departure of manager Fred Westgarth to Hartlepool. Westgarth had joined City from Carlisle in March, 1938 and became a popular figure as he arrested the club's decline. Westgarth was replaced as manager by one of the most remarkable figures in City's history, Councillor Robert Sharp.

Right: Robert Sharp was elected to the City board in February, 1938. During the war his hard work and dedication kept the club alive and Sharp acted as honorary manager for the remainder of the war. In addition to his role at Valley Parade Sharp was twice Councillor for Bradford Moor and deputy Lord Mayor of Bradford in 1945. He also founded Sharp (Floor Furnishings) Ltd. situated to this day in Legrams Lane. When Sharp resigned from the board in 1948 the supporters club presented him with a silver salver and his fellow directors elected him a life member of the club. A record of his time at Valley Parade is provided by the video 'Paraders Past' which features films of City and Valley Parade commissioned by Sharp between 1943 and 1949. This video is available exclusively from Waterstones, Bradford.

In this photograph Councillor Sharp (second from the left) is seen with the City squad at Valley Parade prior to start of the 1946/47 season.

Among the person-alities at Valley Parade were George Hinsley (left) and Frank Shufflebottom (pictured overleaf). Hinsley was City captain until his transfer to Halifax in 1949 and made 120 peacetime appear-ances for the club from 1938. Shufflebottom joined City from Nottingham Forest in 1946 and played 58 times before being appointed trainer in 1949. Bill Murphy (overleaf) joined from Liverpool in 1946 and made 149 appearances in six seasons with the club.

BRADFORD CITY A.F.C.

OFFICIAL TEAM CARD
PRICE 1d.

Bradford City v. Bradford P.A.
Saturday, December 25th, 1943

Bradford City

1 Teasdale
2 Murphy   3 Westlake
(Sheff. W.)
4 Goodyear   5 Beardshaw   6 Lindley
7 Farrington   8 Rodgers or   R. Beattie   9 Deakin   10 Harvey
(Huddsfld)   (Clyde)
11 Bray (Barnsley)

11 Walker   10 Carr   9 A...   8 Shackleton   7 Smith
(Arsenal)   (Leeds...)
6 Farrell   5 Danskin   4 Stabb
5 Compton   2 Stephens
(Arsenal)
Farr

Bradford

To-day sees our last game in the series of League matches. We cannot by any stretch of imagination say that the results have at all been up to the standard we had expected.

We started off fairly well and gained eight points out of the first seven games played. Out of the next ten games played we have had to be satisfied with a paltry three points.

We must say that we were well and truly beaten last Saturday at Park Avenue. We tender our hearty congratulations to the Bradford team on their long run of thirteen games without defeat.

Shall we be able to stop their run of successes to-day? Anyhow we are hoping that our players stretch our visitors to the full. We have not forgotten the ten goals to nil defeat last season and do not want a repetition of that on this occasion.

Next Saturday we start the series of games of the qualification to take part in the draw for the Northern Cup Competition. Barnsley will be our visitors. The games between these old Cup rivals have always been of the most stirring character.

A player who made an impact for City in wartime football was Joe Harvey who was transferred to Newcastle in 1945 and later won FA Cup medals as captain of the Magpies in 1951 and 1952. Harvey went on to manage Newcastle winning the Fairs Cup in 1969 and taking them to the FA Cup Final in 1974.

Murphy (Bradford City)

61 Bradford City

City's last game under wartime arrangements was a 4-2 victory at home to Wrexham on 5 May, 1946. The 1946/47 season marked the return of the conventional league structure and former England international Jack Barker was appointed as manager. In mid-season, after only eight months at Valley Parade, he resigned. Coach Jack Milburn was appointed as City's first player-manager and the club ended the season in a respectable fifth place in Division Three (North). Milburn's reign was a mere eighteen months and in July, 1948 he stepped down to be assistant to allow former Avenue manager David Steele to take over. Steele had been a member of Huddersfield Town's Triple-Championship team of the twenties. In Steele's first season, 1948/49, City finished bottom of Division Three (North) and set an unwanted club record of sixteen games without a win. In 1949/50 they were third from bottom. Although there was a subsequent improvement he could not deliver success at Valley Parade and eventually resigned in February, 1952.

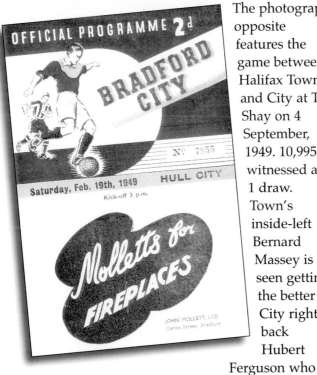

The photograph opposite features the game between Halifax Town and City at The Shay on 4 September, 1949. 10,995 witnessed a 1-1 draw. Town's inside-left Bernard Massey is seen getting the better of City right-back Hubert Ferguson who was one of 40 players to represent the club that season (a record to be beaten in 1996/97). Ferguson played 138 games for City and later joined Halifax Town. The 1948/49 season was one to be forgotten as City finished bottom of Division Three (North). What was notable that season was that 27,083 attended City's game with Hull City at Valley Parade on 19 February, 1949. In the photograph above the City keeper Brendan McManus and defender Jacob Ruecroft clear a Hull attack. Hull finished the season as champions and in the game at Boothferry Park the previous September there was a crowd in excess of thirty-six thousand. City had been beaten 0-2 at Hull but won the return fixture 4-2. The attendance that day remains the highest post-war crowd for a game at Valley Parade. Another point worth commenting on is the design of City's shirt. The claret with amber yoke design had been worn in the 1911 Cup Final and was reintroduced at the start of the season to replace the broad claret and amber stripes which had been worn previously. Unusually for City in this period the shirt had a club crest which was the old Bradford civic coat of arms (as existed between 1907 and 1974). Note also the rugby-style cut of the shirt.

Above: The highlight of the 1949/50 season was the winning of the West Riding Senior Cup on 6 May, 1950. It was the first time that City had won the trophy since 1934. A crowd of 14,372 watched City beat Leeds 3-2 in the final at Valley Parade. In the photograph Dudley is seen beating Brendan McManus in the City goal to open the scoring for Leeds. Frank Greenhoff and Derek Hawksworth (2) scored for City. Bradford born Hawksworth played 75 games for City before his transfer to Sheffield United in December, 1950 where he played 255 League games in the Second and First Division. He returned to Valley Parade in February, 1961 and played a further 44 games for City.

Below and right: The 1950's brought a return of League derbies with Bradford (PA) following Avenue's relegation from Division Two in 1950. In terms of League standing Avenue fared better than City in the first half of the decade although without establishing themselves as serious promotion challengers. In the first derby of the 1950/51 season at Park Avenue on 30 September City were beaten 1-3 with the official attendance stated as 25,655 (the highest post-war derby crowd). In the photograph which was taken from the balcony of the Doll's House at Park Avenue, City forwards Derek Hawksworth and John Millar (in the white change shirts) are waiting for a cross from Ronald Harbertson.

BRADFORD PARK AVENUE

OFFICIAL PROGRAMME

Price 3d

Including SOUVENIR SUPPLEMENT

BRADFORD v. BRADFORD CITY.   SATURDAY, SEPT. 30th. 1950

For All Work in the BUILDING TRADES

Consult

ROBERT RAILTON LTD.

Building and Civil Engineering Contractors

50 EDWARD STREET,   Works: CROFT STREET, BRADFORD

'Phone: 26079

Estimates and Advice Free on Application

In the return game of the 1950/51 season in February, 1951 18,454 watched City beat Avenue 4-1.
Bradford wore their change shirt for this game which was the same design as that worn by Bradford
Northern until fairly recently. Eddie Carr, who scored 56 goals for City in 99 League and Cup games
between 1949-53, is seen beating the Bradford keeper to the ball and passing to Whelan (Polly) Ward
who scored from close range. Carr and Greenhoff (2) scored the other City goals. Ward played 156 games
for City and scored 42 goals. He left City in 1954 to join non-League King's Lynn but signed for Park
Avenue the following year where he established himself as a popular goalscoring inside-forward.

This photograph testifies to the physical nature of the game at the time. City's Ronald Harbertson makes his presence felt in the Hartlepools fixture on 30 December, 1950.

Above: City finished the 1950/51 season in seventh position immediately below Bradford (PA). There were a number of high-scoring victories that season including a 7-0 defeat of Accrington and a 6-0 defeat of New Brighton. Brendan McManus, Bill Murphy and Andrew McGill are featured in this photograph as Barrow make a rare attack on the City goal during the game on 7 October, 1950 which City won 5-1. The old Midland Road and stand is in the background with the club crest on the Kop end gable. The capacity of the stand was cut by 75 per cent following a safety inspection the previous year and a screen was erected to prevent access to the rear of the stand. Another feature worth mentioning is the open 'windows' designed to prevent gale damage and to allow the wind to blow through the stand.

Below: Brendan McManus is beaten by a shot from Carlisle outside-right Hogan in the 2-4 defeat on 21 October, 1950. Eddie Carr, who was second highest scorer in 1950/51 with 13 goals, scored both City's goals.

Above: Valley Parade in June, 1951 with the pitch being re-seeded. This view from the stand was essentially much the same as would have been the case in 1908 when the ground was redeveloped. It was once described as akin to looking from the cockpit of a Sopwith Camel! At the time the stand ran the full length of South Parade and the Bradford end terrace was uncovered. The Midland Road stand was still in existence although the screen which closed off the rear portion (and restricted its capacity to two thousand) is visible. The width of the Paddock would later be reduced as a result of moving the pitch across to provide room for new foundations on the Midland Road side.

THE

PARADER

1951-2

PRICE 1/-

Year Book of
BRADFORD CITY
Shareholders &
Supporters' Association

The crowd await the start of the League game at Valley Parade between City and Oldham Athletic on 29 September, 1951, a game that City won 5-2 in front of 20,746. The photograph is taken at the corner of the old main stand and the Kop with the club's Burlington Terrace offices in the background. The bottom two properties of Burlington Terrace were used as dressing rooms and offices between 1908 and 1961 before final demolition in 1966. A tunnel led from the cellar dressing rooms to the corner of the pitch. The photograph provides a wonderful social commentary on the era and the reader is invited to count the number of female spectators.

Welsh international Ivor Powell was appointed as player-manager in May, 1952 and is seen supervising training on 28 July, 1952. George King and Abe Rosenthal (right) are carrying the balls over the backs of their bemused team mates. Both players were new signings that summer although Liverpool-born Rosenthal was not exactly unfamiliar to the Valley Parade faithful having previously played for City between 1947-49. In 1953-54 he was the club's leading goalscorer (which he had also been in 1947/48). In July 1954 he left City to rejoin Tranmere Rovers from whom City had signed him and then returned to Valley Parade in July 1955 (although he played only once during the 1955/56 season). Rosenthal played for the club as an amateur deriving his income from his lollipop business. Rosenthal and Lee Sinnott (1987, 1993 and 1998) are the only players to have played in three separate spells with Bradford City.

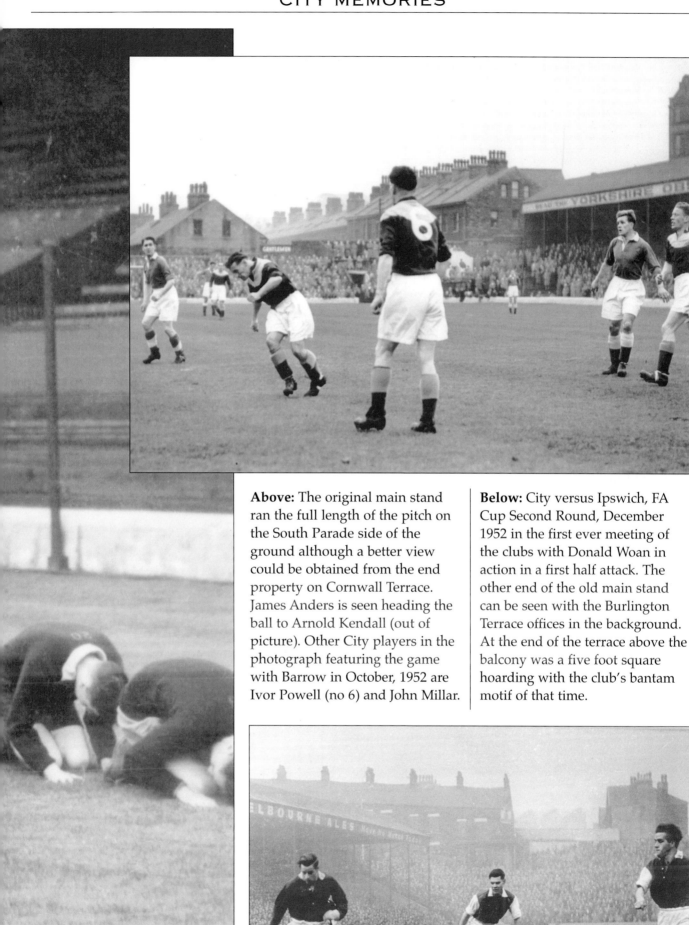

Above: The original main stand ran the full length of the pitch on the South Parade side of the ground although a better view could be obtained from the end property on Cornwall Terrace. James Anders is seen heading the ball to Arnold Kendall (out of picture). Other City players in the photograph featuring the game with Barrow in October, 1952 are Ivor Powell (no 6) and John Millar.

Below: City versus Ipswich, FA Cup Second Round, December 1952 in the first ever meeting of the clubs with Donald Woan in action in a first half attack. The other end of the old main stand can be seen with the Burlington Terrace offices in the background. At the end of the terrace above the balcony was a five foot square hoarding with the club's bantam motif of that time.

Above: Bradford City first team, 25 October, 1952 prior to the game with York City at Valley Parade. Left to right, rear: Jock Whyte, David Gray, Raymond Parker, Brendan McManus and Dick Conroy. Front: Donald Woan, Ivor Powell, Abe Rosenthal, Polly Ward, Jimmy Anders and Arnold Kendall. City finished 16th in Division Three (North) in 1952/53 which will be remembered as the first season in which the club failed to achieve an away win (the only other season was 1989/90). By contrast City established a record of nine successive home wins during the same season.

Below: This photograph shows the Midland Road side after the demolition of the stand in 1952. Left, the Ipswich keeper punches clear from Whelan 'Polly' Ward and Arnold Kendall (no 8). This game was drawn 1-1, the City scorer Denis Close (another City player who developed his reputation elsewhere, albeit in a different sport). City lost the replay 1-5.

Inset: *A shortage of financial resources had implications not only for team strengthening but ground mainte-nance, let alone development and modernisation. During the 1950's the club was forced to operate with what was essentially a three-sided ground. The Midland Road stand was demolished in 1952 and not properly replaced until 1996. Dick Conroy is pictured heading the ball clear during the game with Mansfield in February, 1952. City's Andy McGill, David Gray and Hubert Ferguson are also in the photograph.*

Main picture: *Eddie Carr is seen scoring his 100th peace-time league goal in the game against Carlisle on Easter Tuesday, 1953. Carr scored from a corner by William Tunnicliffe and later completed his hat-trick as City won 7-2. The other City scorers were George Williamson, Whelan Ward and Abe Rosenthal (2).*

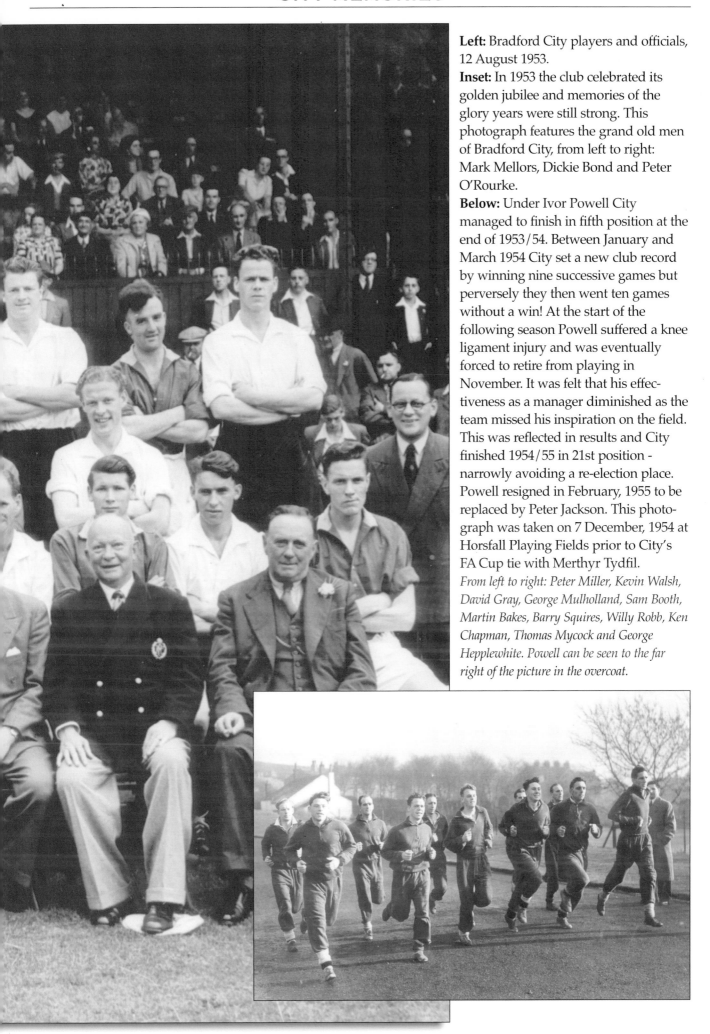

Left: Bradford City players and officials, 12 August 1953.

Inset: In 1953 the club celebrated its golden jubilee and memories of the glory years were still strong. This photograph features the grand old men of Bradford City, from left to right: Mark Mellors, Dickie Bond and Peter O'Rourke.

Below: Under Ivor Powell City managed to finish in fifth position at the end of 1953/54. Between January and March 1954 City set a new club record by winning nine successive games but perversely they then went ten games without a win! At the start of the following season Powell suffered a knee ligament injury and was eventually forced to retire from playing in November. It was felt that his effectiveness as a manager diminished as the team missed his inspiration on the field. This was reflected in results and City finished 1954/55 in 21st position - narrowly avoiding a re-election place. Powell resigned in February, 1955 to be replaced by Peter Jackson. This photograph was taken on 7 December, 1954 at Horsfall Playing Fields prior to City's FA Cup tie with Merthyr Tydfil.

From left to right: Peter Miller, Kevin Walsh, David Gray, George Mulholland, Sam Booth, Martin Bakes, Barry Squires, Willy Robb, Ken Chapman, Thomas Mycock and George Hepplewhite. Powell can be seen to the far right of the picture in the overcoat.

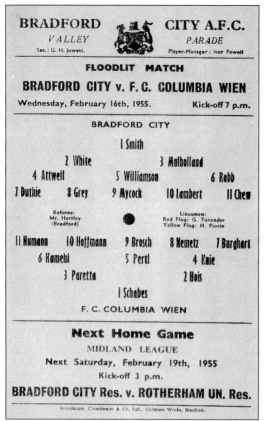

In January, 1955 City met Brentford in the Third Round of the FA Cup. The first game was a 1-1 draw at Brentford and the replay was also drawn, 2-2 after extra-time. **Below:** City's William Robb is seen scoring his side's first goal from the penalty spot. **Right:** A second replay was staged at neutral Highbury where City lost 0-1 in front of a 5,951 crowd. The Brentford keeper is seen punching clear an effort by City's Jackie Chew.

but the Worksop tie was memorable for other reasons. The two teams drew 2-2 when they played at Valley Parade on 10 December, 1955 but City lost the Second Round replay (left) 0-1 five days later. On the next occasion that the Bantams played a non-League side in November, 1957 (below) Scarborough were beaten 6-0 at Valley Parade in the First Round.

Above: The City players are pictured taking a dip at Windsor Baths in preparation for their FA Cup Second Round Replay at Worksop in December, 1955. It was the fourth occasion since the war that City had been paired with a non-League club in the FA Cup at Valley Parade. In 1949 Fleetwood had been beaten 9-0; in 1952 Rhyl Athletic were beaten 4-0 and then in 1954 City beat Merthyr Tydfil 7-1. Older supporters might have recalled the record 11-3 Cup defeat of Walker Celtic in a First Round replay at Valley Parade in December, 1937

OFFICIAL PROGRAMME 3d

BRADFORD CITY

Kick-off 2.30 p.m.

SATURDAY, 19th NOV. 1955   OLDHAM ATHLETIC
F.A. CUP — 1st ROUND

OUR NEXT HOME GAME
MIDLAND LEAGUE
NEXT SATURDAY, NOVEMBER 26th, 1955
BRADFORD CITY v. DONCASTER ROVERS
Kick-off 2.30 p.m.
COME AND GIVE YOUR SUPPORT TO OUR
YOUNGER PLAYERS

TWO DAILY BANKERS
TOP-ALL FLAKE
and
LITTLE TOFF WHIFFS
METCALFE BROS. (Tobacco) LTD.
27-29 WESTGATE · BRADFORD 1

Floodlit Match

BRADFORD CITY v. THIRD LANARK

Monday, October 3rd, 1955.   Kick-off 7.30 p.m.

BRADFORD CITY

1 Smith

2 Whyte   3 Mulholland

4 Gray   5 Williamson   6 Robb

7 Webb   8 Kendall   9 Rosenthal   10 Walsh   11 Simm

Referee:
A. MacFarlane
(Shipley)

Linesmen:
Red Flag—N. M. Copland
White Flag—S. M. Hook

THIRD LANARK

(For Team—see overleaf)

Our Next Home Game

DIVISION III—NORTHERN

SATURDAY, OCTOBER 8th,   Kick-off 3 p.m.

BRADFORD CITY v. CHESTER

JOCK WHYTE SOUVENIR PROGRAMMES WILL BE
ON SALE AT THIS MATCH — PRICE 6d.

Above: Peter Jackson was manager at Bradford City between February 1955 and March 1961 and his era is probably best remembered for a number of famous Cup games. During his first three full seasons in charge City established themselves in the top half of the Third Division (North), culminating with third position in 1958 in the last season of regionalised lower division football. Jackson introduced a youth policy at the club and claimed to have one of the youngest squads in the division. He also gained a reputation for a number of shrewd signings, among them his twin sons Peter and David, Tom Flockett (right back), Bobby Webb (right wing), John McCole (centre forward) and John Reid (inside left). In the photograph he is seen talking to his players after a break in training at Valley Parade in August 1955.

Facing page: City centre-forward Doug Kelly is pictured beating the Oldham left-half in the FA Cup First Round tie at Valley Parade in November, 1955 which City won 3-1 watched by 16,081. City's telegraph pole floodlights were installed the previous year and can be seen in the background as well as the club's claret and amber flag which was flown from the side of the stand on the Kop.

NEWS CHRONICLE AND DISPATCH POCKET PORTRAIT

J. WHYTE
Bradford City F.C.

NEWS CHRONICLE AND DISPATCH POCKET PORTRAIT

P. JACKSON
Bradford City F.C.

NEWS CHRONICLE AND DISPATCH POCKET PORTRAIT

G. WILLIAMSON
Bradford City F.C.

NEWS CHRONICLE AND DISPATCH POCKET PORTRAIT

R. WEBB
Bradford City F.C.

NEWS CHRONICLE AND DISPATCH POCKET PORTRAIT

D. GRAY
Bradford City F.C.

NEWS CHRONICLE AND DISPATCH POCKET PORTRAIT

G. SMITH
Bradford City F.C.

NEWS CHRONICLE AND DISPATCH POCKET PORTRAIT

G. MULLHOLLAND
Bradford City F.C.

NEWS CHRONICLE AND DISPATCH POCKET PORTRAIT

P. JACKSON
Bradford City F.C.

These collectors' cards from the 1955/56 season feature a number of City's key personalities in the 1950's. George Mulholland achieved the record for consecutive League appearances for City playing 231 games between August, 1953 and September, 1958 (246 games if Cup matches are included). Goalkeeper Geoff Smith, ever-present for four seasons 1954 to 1958, holds the record for the most clean sheets, a total of 70 out of 270 games between 1952 and 1959. David Gray was a defender who played for the club between 1948 and 1956 making 257 League and Cup appearances. Full back Jock Whyte (top left) played 251 games between 1950 and 1957 partnered in defence during the same period by George Williamson (top right) who played 235 games for City. The Jackson twins followed their father to Valley Parade from Wrexham after he was appointed manager at City in 1954. Peter played at the back and made 275 League and Cup appearances between March, 1955 and July, 1961. Brother David (top centre) played as a forward/utility player and made 217 appearances during the same period. Peter Jackson senior left City in March, 1961 and his sons were both transferred to Tranmere the following summer.

These photographs from 1955 show the replacement Midland Road shed that was completed in 1954 (and which existed for only six years) as well as the telegraph pole floodlights. Doug Kelly is seen challenging the Halifax Town keeper in the game on 7 September which City won 2-0 with a goal from Kelly and a penalty conversion by John Simm. Kelly was again on the scoresheet for the game with Accrington Stanley on 22 October. In the photograph below Kevin Walsh can be seen beating the offside trap to score City's second goal in the 2-1 victory.

League and Cup games before his transfer to Third Division rivals Swindon in February, 1959.

Above: Twenty-four year old Bill Marshall was signed from Scottish junior club Rutherglen Glencairn in February, 1957 and made his debut in the first team later that season. Marshall played as centre-forward and achieved a good scoring rate for the club with 19 goals in 34

Right: Bradford City players taking glucose as part of their preparation for the FA Cup First Round tie at Derby in November, 1956. The scientific approach obviously had little effect because the Bantams were knocked out of the competition with a 1-2 defeat. John Simm scored City's goal and the attendance for the game was 22,579. Derby had been relegated to the Third Division (North) in 1955, having been relegated from Division One in 1953. In 1955/56 they had been runners-up in Division Three (North) but in 1956/57 they were promoted as champions.

Below: City's Peter Jackson shoots at the Derby County goal during the game on 10 September, 1955 which City won 2-1 with goals from Bobby Webb.

Top: Bradford beat City 4-0 in the derby game at Park Avenue on 22 August, 1953. The photograph shows William Tunnicliffe crossing the ball as Avenue's Jeff Suddards runs in to challenge.

Right and bottom: On Easter Monday, 16 April, 1956 City claimed revenge and recorded their highest League score in a derby game with a 5-0 victory at Valley Parade. The game was played in wet conditions as the photographs testify and the crowd of 11,658 set a record at the time as the lowest for a League game between City and Bradford.

The goals were scored by David Jackson, Peter Jackson, Robert Webb and Les Samuels (two). George Mulholland is seen (above) beating Avenue's Dennis Brickley to the ball with Avenue's Bud Houghton and City's William Robb in close proximity. In the photograph left City's Les Samuels is captured beating Avenue's centre-half Frank Hindle to the ball with David Jackson (10) in what appears to be an offside position.

Above and left: City and Avenue were in the same division (Division Three (North)) for eight seasons during the 1950's, more times in fact than any other decade. Of the 16 derbies City won six and Park Avenue five but it is notable that neither club managed an away win. The games were particularly popular with the Bradford public with attendances averaging around nineteen thousand and six gates were in excess of twenty thousand.

Given that neither side achieved anything during the decade the derbies were the focus of expectation and interest. This photograph features the derby at Park Avenue in October, 1955 when 19,396 witnessed a 1-1 draw. Bradford right-half Dick Conroy (who had transferred from Valley Parade in 1953) and City inside-left Graham Williams are seen in a heading duel watched by Robert Webb (City) and Frank Hindle (Avenue).

OFFICIAL PROGRAMME 3d

BRADFORD CITY A.F.C.

Kick-off 3 p.m.

BRADFORD

Monday, April 16th, 1956

OUR NEXT HOME GAME

DIV. III—NORTHERN

NEXT SATURDAY, APRIL 21st,

CITY v. BARROW

Kick-off 3.15 p.m.

TWO DAILY BANKERS

TOP-ALL FLAKE

and

LITTLE TOFF WHIFFS

METCALFE BROS. (Tobacco) LTD.

57/59 WESTGATE · BRADFORD 1

Wholesale Only

During the last half of the decade City were the top team in Bradford and in 1958 finished third - the highest position achieved by either club during the decade. If City had had a regular goalscorer that season they might have been able to mount a stronger promotion challenge. Avenue had been forced to apply for re-election for the first time in their history in 1956 and it was no secret that they were in financial difficulty. As an attempt to make a fresh start Bradford FC abandoned their traditional red, amber and black and adopted green and white as the club colours. Avenue had worn green and white for a period between 1910 and 1923, originally at the insistence of their new manager Tom Maley who had come from Celtic. They wore green and white as their choice colours in the First Division between 1914 and 1921 (the only club to have ever done so) and it was felt that they might bring a change of fortune 35 years later. Regrettably Bradford couldn't get out of the bottom four of Division Three (North) and so became founder members of Division Four in 1958/59. These photographs feature the derby at Valley Parade in September, 1956 when Avenue were beaten 2-0 by City (who incidentally retained claret and amber through thick, thin and thin from 1903).

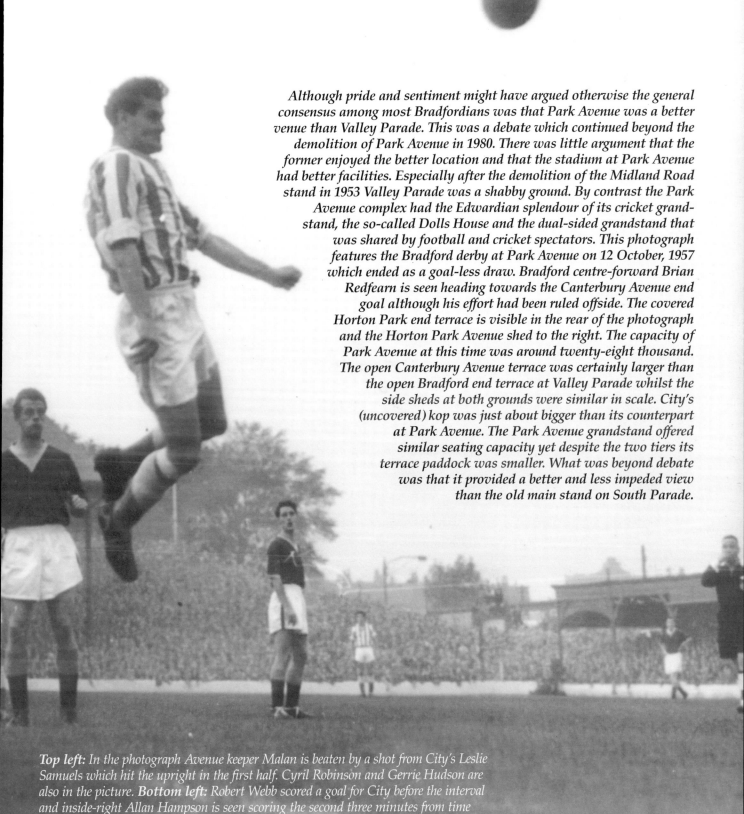

Although pride and sentiment might have argued otherwise the general consensus among most Bradfordians was that Park Avenue was a better venue than Valley Parade. This was a debate which continued beyond the demolition of Park Avenue in 1980. There was little argument that the former enjoyed the better location and that the stadium at Park Avenue had better facilities. Especially after the demolition of the Midland Road stand in 1953 Valley Parade was a shabby ground. By contrast the Park Avenue complex had the Edwardian splendour of its cricket grandstand, the so-called Dolls House and the dual-sided grandstand that was shared by football and cricket spectators. This photograph features the Bradford derby at Park Avenue on 12 October, 1957 which ended as a goal-less draw. Bradford centre-forward Brian Redfearn is seen heading towards the Canterbury Avenue end goal although his effort had been ruled offside. The covered Horton Park end terrace is visible in the rear of the photograph and the Horton Park Avenue shed to the right. The capacity of Park Avenue at this time was around twenty-eight thousand. The open Canterbury Avenue terrace was certainly larger than the open Bradford end terrace at Valley Parade whilst the side sheds at both grounds were similar in scale. City's (uncovered) kop was just about bigger than its counterpart at Park Avenue. The Park Avenue grandstand offered similar seating capacity yet despite the two tiers its terrace paddock was smaller. What was beyond debate was that it provided a better and less impeded view than the old main stand on South Parade.

Top left: In the photograph Avenue keeper Malan is beaten by a shot from City's Leslie Samuels which hit the upright in the first half. Cyril Robinson and Gerrie Hudson are also in the picture. *Bottom left:* Robert Webb scored a goal for City before the interval and inside-right Allan Hampson is seen scoring the second three minutes from time (below left). The crowd that day was 20,513.

Chapter four
Times of hope and despair
1958 - 1983

Below: City and Avenue met on three occasions in the FA Cup and each of the games was played at Park Avenue. The first of those games had been in February, 1912 when City, as holders of the FA Cup, beat Avenue 1-0 in the Third Round watched by 24,833 spectators. The remaining games were both in the 1950's. In December, 1951 Avenue beat City 3-2 in a Second Round tie in front of 24,430 but in December, 1958 it was City who were the victors with a crowd of 19,962 witnessing their 2-0 Second Round win. Centre forward John McCole is captured in the process of scoring his second goal.

McCole had been signed from Falkirk in September, 1958 and during his first season at Valley Parade scored 28 times in 34 League games (to set a new club record) and also managed six goals in four FA Cup ties. McCole played eight games for City during the 1959/60 season and scored four goals. His remarkable scoring rate attracted the interest of other clubs and in September 1959 he left to join First Division Leeds. McCole did not find the transition from Third Division football particularly difficult and scored 22 in 33 games although he could not prevent his new club being relegated. He made a further 45 appearances for Leeds in Division Two scoring 23 goals before rejoining Fourth Division City in October, 1961. During 1961/62 McCole scored ten times in 26 games alongside new goalscoring hero David Layne (who was transferred to Sheffield Wednesday during the 1962 close season). The following season City struggled at the foot of the League and

McCole scored only five times in 20 games before his transfer to Third Division Rotherham. McCole was later replaced by Rod Green from Bradford (PA) who established his own goal-scoring reputation with 39 goals from 66 games during the second half of the 1962/63 season (10 goals) and during 1963/64 (29). It was not until 1975/76 that City had a forward who scored more than twenty League goals in a season (Joe Cooke, 22). **Below right:** In this photograph McCole is seen scoring the first goal of his hat-trick against Southend at Valley Parade on 28 March, 1959 in a game which City won 6-1.

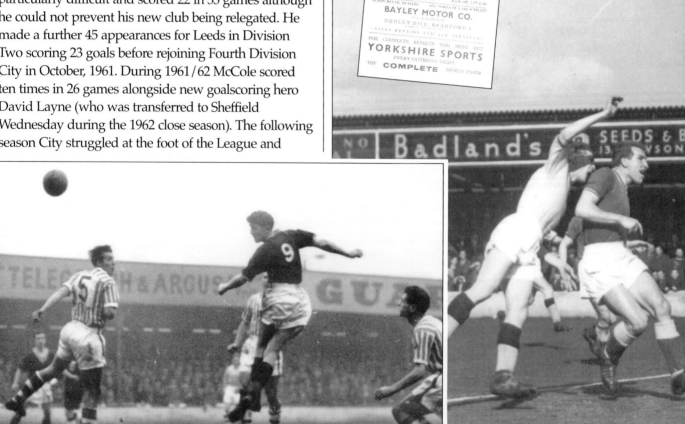

Derek Stokes was another goalscoring hero who emerged at this time. Signed as a junior in 1956 he made his debut at Crewe in September, 1957 where he scored twice in City's 2-2 draw. The foll-owing season, 1958/59, he was virt-ually ever-present and scored 15 goals in 45 games making an effective partnership with John McCole. In 1959/60 he scored 25 goals in 37 games for City before joining Second Division Huddersfield Town where he was consistently their top scorer. Stokes rejoined City at the start of the 1966 season but made only 17 League and Cup appearances with three goals to his credit. Stokes is second from the left on the front row in this photograph of Bradford City during the 1959/60 season. *Other players featured are (left to right from the back) D.Jackson, Roberts, Lawlor, Downie, Mulholland, P.Jackson, Webb, Stokes, Flockett, Reid and Boyle.*

City reached the Fourth Round of the FA Cup in 1958/59 for the first time in 23 years, beaten at First Division Preston in front of 35,716 fans. The following season they played a total of eight games in the FA Cup, albeit including three replays. Derek Stokes is seen above scoring City's winner against Rochdale in the Second Round replay at Valley Parade. In the Third Round City caused a major upset by beating First Division Everton 3-0 at Valley Parade in front of a 23,550 crowd. **Below:** City captain Tom Flockett pictured receiving treatment prior to the next Cup game. Nearly twenty thousand watched City overcome Bournemouth in the Fourth Round to earn a Fifth Round home draw with Division One leaders (and eventual champions) Burnley. A capacity 26,227 crowd saw Robert Webb and David Stokes put City into a 2-0 lead with only 15 minutes remaining. Burnley pulled a goal back and then managed an equaliser in the final minute of injury time. In the photograph on the facing page keeper George Stewart gathers the ball with City no.4 Bernard Devitt in support. City lost 0-5 in the replay at Turf Moor. The attendance for that game was 52,850 with a large contingent from Bradford and stories of traffic tailbacks as far as Shipley! Defeat at Burnley saw an end to a 19 game unbeaten run but the Bantams lost ten of their 16 remaining games to finish 19th in Division Three.

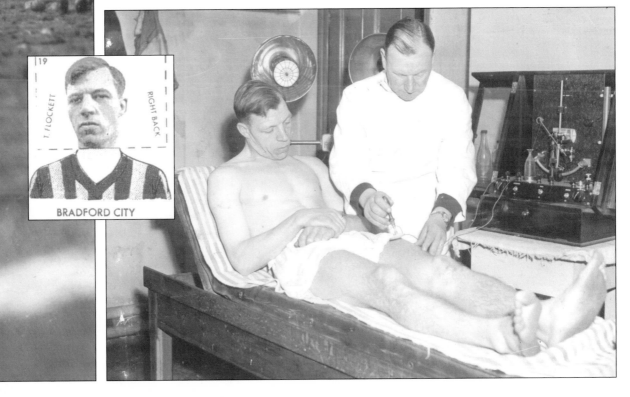

19
T. FLOCKETT   RIGHT BACK

BRADFORD CITY

Right: City were relegated from Division Three at the end of 1960/61 when they finished in 22nd position. Moving in the opposite direction were Bradford (PA) (enjoying their third and final promotion season whilst members of the League between 1907 and 1970). Failure in the League caused manager Peter Jackson to resign in March, 1961 but the season was notable for a famous League Cup victory over Manchester United. City beat their First Division opponents 2-1 at Valley Parade on 2 November, 1960 in front of a small midweek afternoon crowd of 4,670. At the time of the game City had managed to win three out of 15 League games and three days later could only draw 0-0 with non-League Scarborough in a First Round FA Cup tie at Valley Parade (the replay of that game was won 3-1 after extra time).

Two teams on the cover every week
SOCCER STAR
BRADFORD CITY 1960 Left to right (back): Jackson (P.), Lawlor, Downie, Currie, Mollatt. (Front), Webb, Jackson (D.), Flockett, Howard, Reid, Duncan (W.1)

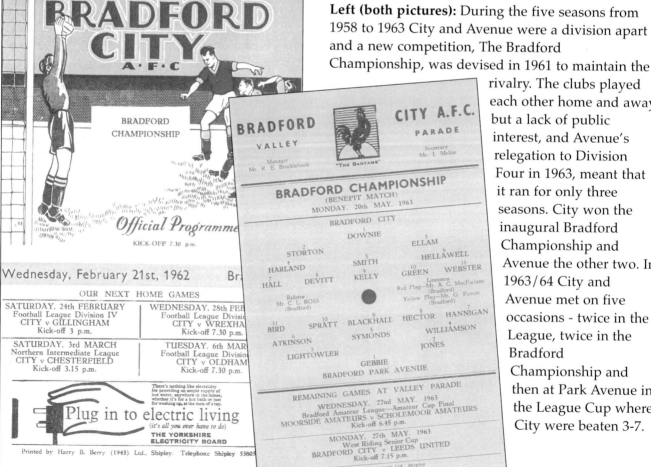

Left (both pictures): During the five seasons from 1958 to 1963 City and Avenue were a division apart and a new competition, The Bradford Championship, was devised in 1961 to maintain the rivalry. The clubs played each other home and away but a lack of public interest, and Avenue's relegation to Division Four in 1963, meant that it ran for only three seasons. City won the inaugural Bradford Championship and Avenue the other two. In 1963/64 City and Avenue met on five occasions - twice in the League, twice in the Bradford Championship and then at Park Avenue in the League Cup where City were beaten 3-7.

Above: Bradford City finished the 1961/62 season in fifth place despite having been fifth from bottom at the end of January. The club won 15 and drew two of their last 19 games which included a run of seven successive wins. City needed to win their last two games to secure promotion but were beaten 3-5 in the penultimate fixture at Workington. Promotion rivals Wrexham were defeated in the last game of the season but City missed out on promotion by a single point. That season City scored 94 goals and conceded 86. Nine of those goals were scored by Colchester in the away game on 30 December 1961 when City suffered their record League defeat, 1-9 (ironically the Bantams had beaten Colchester 4-1 at Valley Parade four days previously). In the FA Cup City were beaten 0-1 in the Third Round by Arsenal at Highbury.

Below: The photograph shows the Christmas party held at chairman Herbert Munro's house in 1961. John McCole is stood to the left of Munro with his hand on the table. Immediately behind Munro is David Layne. Malcolm Currie, captain Tom Flockett and manager Bob Brocklebank are seated in the foreground. Brocklebank had been appointed in May, 1961 and remained with the club until October, 1964.

Other individuals present included Jimmy Lawlor (far left), Mike Smith (fifth from left) and Ron Mollatt, Stan Harland, Stan Storton, Bernard Devitt and Derek Hawksworth (stood centre, left to right).

One player who did not feature in the photograph was Trevor Hockey who had been sold to Nottingham Forest in November, 1961 for a then record fee of £15,000. Hockey had made his debut during the 1959/60 season and made 53 League appearances before his transfer. Hockey had had an England Youth trial in 1959 but much later won nine full caps as a Welsh international despite his Keighley birthplace. Hockey returned to Valley Parade in 1974 to make 43 League appearances. In January, 1962 a smallpox epidemic was declared in Bradford which led to a postponement of home matches.

In 1961/62 David 'Bronco' Layne set a new club record with 34 goals from 43 matches. Layne had been signed from then Third Division rivals Swindon Town in December 1960 but his ten goals in 22 League games had been unable to prevent relegation. During the 1962 close season he was sold for a club record £22,500 to First Division Sheffield Wednesday where he scored 52 goals in 74 League games. David Layne subsequently achieved notoriety for his involvement in a match rigging scandal and received a life ban from the game from the Football Association.

The winter of 1962/63 was particularly severe and City went without a game for ten weeks. When they finally played the first game of 1963, against Newcastle in the Third Round of the FA Cup, they were beaten 1-6 at Valley Parade (a memorable game for eighteen year old England Youth international Dave Roper in goal). City won only four out of 22 League games between March and May, 1963 and finished second to bottom of Division Four. Most supporters blamed the sale of key players and the lack of investment in the side (much of the money received had been spent on Valley Parade itself) and this generated a certain amount of cynicism that City were an unambitious 'selling' club.

During the club's last season in Division Three (North), when City were among the front runners, attendances at Valley Parade averaged twelve and a half thousand. Following relegation to Division Four in 1961 gates averaged well below half this level. In 1962/63 there were four games which attracted fewer than two thousand spectators to Valley Parade with only 1,733 in attendance for the last home game of the season against York City. In 1963/64 the average attendance was 5,739 despite the fact that City were challenging for a promotion place. In fact City had two gates of under three thousand that season but also enjoyed two five figure attendances: 12,164 for the visit of Bradford (relegated from Division Three the previous year) and 17,974 for the visit of Workington. The latter was the highest attendance for a League game at Valley Parade since 1958 and has yet to be exceeded. City had to beat Workington (who were level on points) to win promotion but they lost 0-2. In the last game of the season City were defeated 0-1 at York and finished in fifth place.

Bradford City at Chester 9 November, 1963. From left to right, back row: Kelly (2), Wragg (4), Fisher (1), Smith (5), Ellam (3) and Hall (7). Front row: Green (9), Stowell (8), Harland (captain, no.6), Price (10) and Thorpe (11).

Above: In the eight seasons 1962/63 to 1969/70 inclusive a Bradford club finished in the bottom two of Division Four on no less than six occasions. At the end of 1962/63 and 1965/66 Bradford City were forced to apply for re-election, having finished in 23rd position. In 1964/65 City narrowly avoided applying for re-election when they finished 19th. In 1966/67 City finished in a mid-table position but Bradford (PA) were 23rd and they spent the next three seasons at the bottom of the division before losing their League place to Cambridge United in 1970. Coinciding with the rise of Don Revie's 'Super Leeds' it was sad but not altogether surprising that many Bradfordians turned their backs on City and Avenue and drifted east. City had a reputation for being a 'selling-club' and it did not build goodwill with supporters. The abysmal record of the two clubs also made wealthy benefactors unwilling to inject new capital into either of them. The story of the sixties was thus a struggle for survival and many people questioned whether Bradford could support two League clubs.

Above: Stafford Heginbotham is pictured with manager Willie Watson, Derek Stokes and Ken Leek (left) in April, 1966. Stokes returned to Valley Parade from Huddersfield in an exchange for Roy Ellam in 1966. Welsh international Ken Leek was the club's £10,000 record signing in November, 1965 and the club's leading

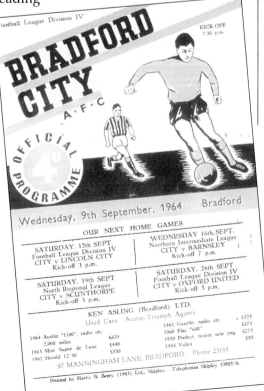

goalscorer with 11 goals in 1965/66. Leek made 104 League and Cup appearances for City and scored 26 goals in his three seasons at Valley Parade. Watson did much to get the club moving and out of the doldrums and deserves credit for the revival of Bradford City in the late sixties.

In 1964 Bradford City reached the Fifth Round of the League Cup after a surprise 1-0 victory at Second Division Charlton. Later that month they were beaten 0-1 at home in the First Round of the FA Cup by Scarborough and 1-7 at Aston Villa in the League Cup.

Right: In 1966 there were two fairly significant changes to the ground. The open Bradford end terrace was finally covered and the club's former offices and dressing rooms at the bottom of Burlington Terrace (on the north west corner of the kop) were demolished. The current office and dressing room complex at the corner of the main stand and Bradford end was constructed in 1961 and it is now the oldest surviving part of Valley Parade. A plan in 1963 to erect a glass fibre roof over the kop never got off the drawing board.

Right: Average gates of around four and a half thousand during the mid-sixties including a then record low of 1,353 for the visit of Wrexham in May, 1966 had an inevitable impact on finances. In January, 1967 Stafford Heginbotham staged the famous crisis meeting at St Georges Hall in the hope of raising new funds. Heginbotham's enthusiasm was significant in safeguarding the future of Bradford City and energising supporters. Probably the biggest difference between City and Park Avenue was that the former had a chairman with commitment and initiative. Ultimately Heginbotham would be able to boast four seasons of successive improvement from 23rd in Division Four in 1966 to 10th in Division Three in 1970 and a doubling of gates during the same period. The club also had to thank individual supporters for its survival. This picture features Heginbotham with Baildon branch members Alan and Gladys Hannah,

Geoff Collinson (right) and Harry Jones (seated). Long-serving Bradford City Secretary Jim Mellor is in the background. There were many others who helped with fund raising and it was tragic that Sam Firth, who did so much for the club, perished in the disaster in 1985 at the age of 86 and never saw his beloved Bradford City back in Division Two.

Manager Bill Harris resigned in the spring of 1966 after only one year in charge as City struggled at the bottom of Division Four. Performances had been disappointing since the beginning of the 1965/66 season with successive 1-7 defeats against Crewe (away) and Stockport (home) being cases in point. Stafford Heginbotham took charge as chairman in October, 1965 and appointed a new manager, a former England cricket and football international, Willie Watson in April, 1966. Inspired by the football marketing strategies which emerged in World Cup year Heginbotham was not frightened to introduce his own ideas to promote Bradford City. One of those was the redesign of the club programme in March, 1966 and the introduction of the City Gent character (a caricature of Heginbotham) on its cover. Heginbotham tried without much success to attract commercial sponsorship including the offer of life membership of the club for one hundred guineas. This photograph was taken in July, 1968 when Heginbotham opened his house to the public. Pictured left to right are Ian Cooper, Bruce Stowell and triallist keeper David Pollard.

Above: Wrexham had been beaten 7-1 at Valley Parade in the First Round of the FA Cup in December, 1967 and the City squad are pictured preparing for the Second Round game with Bury in January, 1968 (which they lost 0-1). From left to right: Pat Liney, Bruce Stowell, Arthur Taylor, John Hall, Tom Hallett, Ken Leek, Charlie Rackstraw, Ian Cooper, Alex Smith and Wilf Shergold. Three first-team players not included were Ernie Swallow, Bruce Bannister and Paul Aimson.

The 1967/68 season was the third that decade in which City missed promotion by one place. When City entertained Bradford on 10 February, 1968 they were at the top of Division Four and Avenue were at the bottom.

However the visitors won the game 2-1 to record their only away win of the season and ultimately their last in the Football League. The final game of 1967/68 was a home fixture against Doncaster Rovers and City needed to get a better result than Crewe that day to go up. In the previous game City had beaten Champions-elect Luton 3-1 and so became the only team to beat them at home that season. Against mid-table Doncaster however City could only manage a 1-1 draw. Just before the end of the game a rumour spread around Valley Parade that Crewe had lost and many people in the 12,478 crowd ran onto the pitch to congratulate the team. Chairman Stafford Heginbotham was obliged to announce over the tannoy that Crewe had actually won and so the celebrations were cancelled!

During 1968 City had no fewer than three changes of manager. Willie Watson, who had been appointed by chairman Stafford Heginbotham in April 1966, resigned in January. He was quickly succeeded by thirty-six year old former Leeds full-back Grenville Hair who sadly collapsed and died after a training session on 7 March. Coach Jim McAnearney and skipper Tom Hallett then shared the duties before Jimmy Wheeler was appointed in June.

Below: 1968/69 will be remembered as the season in which Bradford City managed to achieve promotion from Division Four. At the end of 1968 City had won only eight out of 27 League and Cup games and were in 13th position. The club began the new year by securing their second away win of the season but it was to be the start of a 21 game unbeaten run which lifted City into a promotion place. One of the men responsible for this turn of form was Norman Corner who made his debut in the goal-less draw at Park Avenue in January, 1969 in what would be the last Bradford League derby. Defeat at Brentford in the penultimate game ended the unbeaten run and meant that City had to beat promotion rivals Darlington at Feethams on the last day of the season. The large contingent of supporters who travelled from Bradford witnessed a thrilling 3-1 victory which resulted in City's first promotion success for 40 years. It was a great achievement for manager Jimmy Wheeler who had been appointed less than twelve months before. A notable statistic is that City drew a club record 20 out of 46 League games in 1968/69.

Below: The City squad is pictured at the start of the promotion season. Back row, left to right: Bobby Ham, Ron Bayliss, Bruce Stowell, Pat Liney, John Roberts, John Hall, Ian Cooper, Barry Swallow. Front: Tony Leighton, Gerry Lightowler, Arthur Taylor, Charlie Rackstraw, Tom Hallett, Bruce Bannister, Peter Middleton and Bruce Walker.

Above: The Paraders made a great start to their first season back in Division Three after an eight year absence and at the end of 1969 the club was in third place. Out of forty-six League games played in 1969 City lost six and these were all away from home (one of which was a 0-5 defeat at leaders Luton on 13 December). City had enjoyed a good run in the League Cup which included a giant-killing at First Division Sunderland in the Second Round and an eventual defeat in the Fourth Round at West Brom. In the FA Cup City had reached the Third Round where they were awarded a home tie against Tottenham Hotspur. The game is remembered as one of the greatest Cup ties at Valley Parade with Bobby Ham and Bruce Stowell each scoring to secure a 2-2 draw. City were crushed 0-5 in the replay at White Hart Lane but January, 1970 is memorable also for City's 8-1 victory over Bournemouth at Valley Parade which remains the club's highest post-war victory and which extended the sequence of unbeaten home games to 23. What was remarkable about the second half of the season was that City managed only four wins out of 23 games as their form took a nosedive. City suffered two successive home defeats after the Bournemouth game and managed only one more home win.

Bradford City 1969/70. Back row: Atkins, Stowell, Oliver (trainer), Cooper and Rackstraw. Middle: Corner, McConnell, Hall, Liney, Roberts, Bayliss, Turbitt and Swallow. Front: Steward, Bannister, Ham, Wheeler (manager), Hallett, Leighton and Middleton.

football. Bruce Stowell actually broke the existing 55 year old appearance record in 1970 and went on to appear in 401 League games for City between 1960 and 1972. John Hall broke Bruce Stowell's record in 1974 with 417 appearances between 1962 and 1974 and then Ian Cooper set a new record in 1976 before reaching a total of 442 appearances between 1965 and 1977. Terry Owen, father of England's World Cup hero Michael Owen, is also in the photograph.

Above: City's indifferent form continued into 1970/71. A lack of finance restricted squad strengthening and forced the sale of Bobby Ham to Preston in October, 1970. The team was generally unchanged from the previous campaign and included four players who would each achieve a place in the record books as a result of representing the club in League competition more than four hundred times. Ces Podd made his debut in 1970 and went on to make a record 502 League appearances before joining Halifax Town in August, 1984. Podd was a popular club man but is also remembered as one of the first black players to establish himself in English

Bradford City, 1970/71 from left to right, back row: Kaye (physio), McHale, Podd, Liney, Ritchie, Corner, Oates and Cooper. Middle row: Rooks, Bannister, Owen, Stowell, Wilson (acting manager), Middleton, Hall.C, Hall.J, O'Neill and Howell. Front row: Flynn, Exley, Cooke, Longstaff and Boshell.

Top: In June, 1969 Bradford City participated in a twin-towns football tournament in Roubaix, France. Bobby Ham and Bruce Bannister did not participate and City inevitably missed their striking power. Borussia Moenchengladbach were beaten 2-1 but City lost 0-1 against Roubaix.

Bobby Ham, scorer of a hat-trick against Bournemouth on 24 January, 1970. Bradford born Ham played for both Avenue and City during a 14 year career in which he scored 156 goals in 460 League appearances. He played 187 League games for City between February, 1968 and October, 1970 and then August, 1973 to May, 1975 scoring a total of 64 League goals for the Paraders. Ham made 109 consecutive League appearances between April 1968 and October 1970. Whilst at Park Avenue he had partnered Kevin Hector.

Above: In February, 1972 as City struggled against relegation Bryan Edwards sought to impose tighter discipline with a restriction on long hair. However this training photograph taken six months later testifies that few took any notice. From left to right: Johnnie Johnson, Gerry Ingram, Warren Rayner, John Hall, Tommy Hale, Joe Cooke, Ian Cooper, John Middleton, Ronnie Brown and John Ritchie.

Attendances averaged just under nine thousand during the 1969/70 season (the highest level for ten years) but fell to around five thousand as the team became involved in a relegation struggle. Back in Division Four in 1972 the gates deteriorated further, averaging under three and a half thousand for the first time in the club's history. The last game of the 1974/75 season was watched by only 1,697 and in 1975/76

average League gates fell to a record low of 2,916 with two attendances of under two thousand. Needless to say the club had to operate under extreme financial constraints and once again this was the dominant theme for the decade. Bradford (PA) vacated Park Avenue in May 1973 and spent a season as tenants at Valley Parade before going into liquidation. City supporters resisted the suggestion of merger and a new Bradford Metro FC identity. In January, 1974 the Bob Martin era begin when he replaced Stafford Heginbotham as chairman with Messrs Dunne, Morrison, Tordoff and Wilkinson joining the board as directors. Martin made his impact by taking the City Gent character from the front of the programme and introducing a predominantly white strip (which certainly endeared him to the supporters).

Below: Having narrowly avoided relegation in 1971 City finished the 1971/72 season in the bottom position of Division Three. Manager Jimmy Wheeler was sacked at the end of September, 1971 and Ray Wilson (a member of the 1966 England World Cup winning team) acted as caretaker for a month until the eventual appointment of Bryan Edwards who began an association with the club that would continue until quite recently. Financial pressure meant that City could not refuse a record offer of £23,000 from Bristol Rovers for Bruce Bannister, former scoring partner of Bobby Ham. Earlier in the season Rovers had beaten City 7-1 at Eastville. Bannister (pictured scoring against Barnsley in April, 1968) played 218 League and Cup games and scored 68 goals for City having made his debut in September, 1965. Gerry Ingram was subsequently signed from Preston as Bannister's replacement (along with full back John Ritchie) in March, 1972 but by then relegation was almost inevitable. Relegation was a great disappointment and a lost opportunity for City to establish themselves as a formidable team now that they were sole representatives of the city of Bradford. The subsequent drop in gates at Valley Parade reflected the sense of disillusionment among the Bradford public. With Avenue struggling to make an impact in the Northern Premier League many Bradfordians looked instead to the likes of Burnley, Leeds or Manchester United for a team to follow.

Bryan Edwards spent three seasons at Valley Parade trying to achieve promotion from Division Four and although City climbed within reach of a promotion place in March, 1974 they finished in eighth position. In 1974/75 he brought Trevor Hockey back to the club for a then record £12,500 from Aston Villa but the move was not a success and Hockey missed half the season through injury.

In January, 1975 Edwards admitted defeat and resigned. Although he had failed to deliver League success his reign will be remembered for the fact that City reached the Fourth Round of the FA Cup in two successive seasons, a feat that had been achieved only twice before during the post-war period. In 1973 City defeated Second Division Blackpool 2-1 at Valley Parade in the Third Round

Gerry Ingram made a total of 171 League appearances for City and scored 60 goals in his six seasons with the club between March, 1972 and February, 1977. He is remembered for the striking partnerships he formed with Allan Gilliver in 1972/73 and 1973/74 and then with Bobby Ham who returned to Valley Parade in 1974/75. In December, 1972 Ingram scored four goals (including two penalties) in the 7-0 defeat of Darlington at Valley Parade. During his last two seasons with City Ingram partnered Joe Cooke who had moved from centre-half to centre-forward at the start of the 1975/76 season.

Bradford City 1974/75 from left to right, rear: Bobby Kennedy (Youth Coach), Colin Kaye (Physio), John Napier, Ces Podd, Gerry Ingram, Peter Downsborough, Ian Cooper, John Middleton, Joe Cooke and Bryan Edwards. Front: Ronnie Brown, Rod Johnson, Bobby Ham, Trevor Hockey, Don Hutchins and Garry Watson.

(both goals scored by former Blackpool striker Gerry Ingram) with the reward of a trip to Highbury where Arsenal beat them 2-0. The following season City beat Fourth Division rivals Workington and Barnsley before being drawn at home to non-League Alvechurch at Valley Parade in the Third Round. The tie is memorable for the fact that it was the first competitive first-team game to be played at Valley Parade on a Sunday (special dispensation was provided by the Football Association in view of the exceptional circumstances arising from the power strikes and the three day working week). TV advertising helped attract a 13,062 crowd (double the size expected) and City's 4-2 victory earned a Fourth Round tie at Luton where they were beaten 0-3.

Above: Bryan Edwards had been obliged to operate on a shoestring but introduced a number of players who became firm favourites at Valley Parade including Rod Johnson from Rotherham United (above), Peter Downsborough from Swindon, John Napier from Brighton, Don Hutchins from Blackburn and John Middleton (brother of Peter Middleton who was a first-teamer between 1968 and 1972). David Fretwell emerged from the reserves to establish himself as a regular in the team and Garry Watson was given his debut in 1972. Edwards should ultimately be given credit for laying the foundations of the side that finally achieved promotion in 1977 under Bobby Kennedy.

Right: Graham Oates is credited as the scorer of the fastest recorded goal in City's history after 17 seconds on 14 November, 1973 against Mansfield. A Bradfordian, he made 158 League appearances for City between 1969 and 1974 before signing for Blackburn and then Newcastle. Oates is photographed with Ian Cooper at Valley Parade on 26 May, 1977 for the occasion of Cooper's testimonial game.

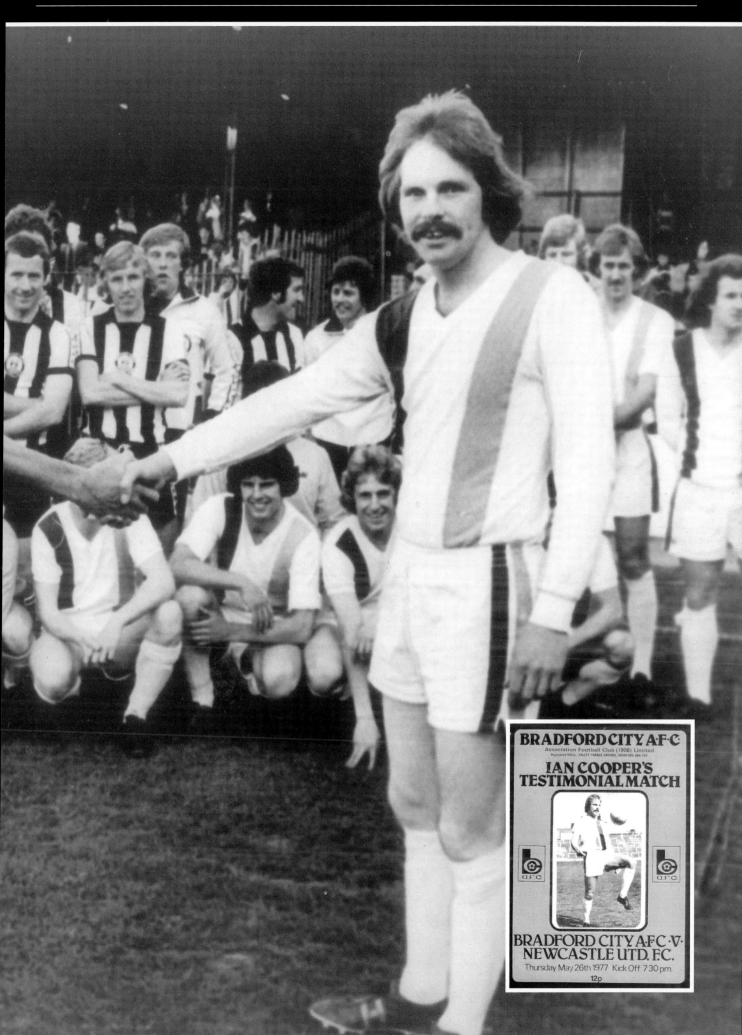

BRADFORD CITY A·F·C·
Association Football Club (1908) Limited
Registered Office: VALLEY PARADE GROUND, BRADFORD BD8 7DY

IAN COOPER'S TESTIMONIAL MATCH

BRADFORD CITY A·F·C· ·V· NEWCASTLE UTD. FC.
Thursday May 26th 1977 Kick Off 7.30 pm.

12p

Football Association Challenge Cup
6th Round

BRADFORD CITY
versus
SOUTHAMPTON

SATURDAY 6th MARCH 1976
Kick-Off 3 p.m.

b.a.f.c.

5th Round : Winning goal at Norwich   Photograph by courtesy of Telegraph & Argus

Souvenir Programme 20p

Above: The 1975/76 season is remembered for City's exploits in the FA Cup and the achievement of reaching the Sixth Round. The Cup run saved the club from insolvency, rekindled interest in Bradford City and generated a momentum that resulted in promotion the following year. In March, 1975 City had considered a plan to go part-time and prior to the start of the 1975/76 season drastic economies had been made to the payroll with the departure of Bobby Ham, John Napier and Ronnie Brown. The average age of the squad was particularly young and included the likes of David Hall (21 years), Billy McGinley (20), Joe Cooke (20), Dave Fretwell (23), John Middleton (20), Ces Podd (23), David Ratcliffe (18), Gary Watson (19) and Clive McFadzean (17). The men with experience were Ian Cooper, Rod Johnson, Gerry Ingram, Trevor Hockey, Don Hutchins and goalkeeper Peter Downsborough. The team struggled all season to avoid a re-election position in the bottom four and eventually finished 17th. In this context the Cup run was all the more remarkable.

Above right: In 1976 Bradford City reached the last eight of the FA Cup for the first time since 1920 and it remains a feat that has not been repeated. In the First Round Chesterfield were beaten 1-0 at Valley Parade. Away wins at Rotherham (3-0) and then Shrewsbury (2-1) led to a Fourth Round home tie with non-League Tooting & Mitcham which City won 3-1 in front of a 21,152 crowd. City were then drawn away at First Division Norwich in the Fifth

Round where they achieved the giant-killing of the season by winning 2-1 against the run of play. Billy McGinley scored the winner at Norwich with Don Hutchins having given City a first half lead. Hutchins scored five goals during the Cup run (he managed only six out of 38 League appearances that season) and is pictured with Joe Cooke during the Sixth Round tie with Southampton at Valley Parade. City fought bravely against their Second Division opponents but it was a controversial goal that earned the eventual Cup winners Southampton a place in the Semi-Finals.

Above: Proceeds from the Cup run allowed the signing of right-back Peter Hardcastle and Terry Dolan from Huddersfield (and formerly of Bradford (PA)). Between 1976 and 1981 Dolan played 217 League and Cup games for City, the club he had supported as a boy, and as manager he came close to getting City promoted to Division One in 1988. Bradford City were among the front runners in Division Four from the start of the 1976/77 season. During the second half of the campaign Bernie Wright was signed from Walsall as a replacement for Gerry Ingram and Phil Nicholls from Crewe to strengthen the defence. Promotion was secured with a 1-1 draw at home to Bournemouth in the penultimate game (the goal scored by Joe Cooke) and City finished the season in fourth place with an unbeaten home record.

Bradford City 1976/77 from left to right, rear: Bobby Kennedy, Ron Barritt (Physio), Ces Podd, Dave Ratcliffe, Terry Dolan, Joe Cooke, Peter Downsborough, Warren Rayner, Peter Hardcastle, Ian Cooper, David Hall, John Middleton, John Napier (Player Coach). Front: Tibor Szabo, Graham Jones, Dave Fretwell, Billy McGinley, Rod Johnson, Gerry Ingram, Garry Watson, Don Hutchins and Eugene Martinez.

Below: Kennedy kept faith with the team that had won promotion (in large measure because the funds were not available for new signings). City got off to a great start in 1977/78 with a 4-0 win over Cambridge who had been promoted as Fourth Division Champions and who were promoted again at the end of the season as runners-up. The victory extended the club's sequence of unbeaten home League games to a record 25 dating back to May, 1976. The next win however was not forthcoming until the end of September and City struggled at the bottom of the Third Division all season, handicapped by very poor away form which included ten successive away defeats. Kennedy was replaced at the end of January by John Napier. Funds generated from City's successful new lottery were made available for team strengthening and the following month the club record outgoing transfer fee was broken twice in the same day: £15,000 was paid to Blackburn for defender Mick Wood and then £25,000 to Leeds for striker David McNiven. Centre-half Steve Baines was later signed from Huddersfield. Sadly they could not prevent the club being relegated after only one season in Division Three.

Bradford City July, 1977 from left to right: Nicholls, Downsborough, Cooke, Dolan, Wright, Spark, Hutchins, Podd, Watson, Middleton, Fretwell, Hardcastle and Johnson.

K. Tempest

final 21 games of the season and was on the losing side only three times. Les Chapman was an influential signing in February, 1980 and served the club as a winger and a full back during his four seasons with City. A defeat at Peterborough on the last day of the season cost City promotion (on goal difference despite the fact that City conceded only 14 goals at home all season) and once more the Paraders finished fifth in Division Four.

Bradford City, 1979/80. From left to right, back row: Robertson, Jackson, Burton, Smith, Wood, Gallagher and Reaney. Middle: Mulhall (manager), Kaye (physio), Cooper, Watson, Hutchins, Podd, Dolan and Edwards (coach). Front row: Baines, Bailey, Bates, McNiven, Martinez and Staniforth.

Top: City started the 1979/80 season with an eight game unbeaten run that included seven wins and which took City to the top of Division Four. The run ended at Wigan where City were soundly beaten 1-4. The squad had been strengthened by the close season signings of Terry Cooper from Lincoln and Dave Staniforth from Bristol Rovers who both made a big contribution to the team. Another man who made an instant impact was Bobby Campbell who joined the club on a trial basis in December, 1979. Campbell played in each of the

Above left: Peter Downsborough played 650 League games (the first goalkeeper in League history to do so) of which 225 were for City between 1973 and 1979. The highlight of his career was winning the League Cup with Swindon in 1969. At Valley Parade he developed a reputation for penalty saving whilst team mate Terry Dolan had the reputation for penalty taking.

Below: During the 1978 close season former Leeds players Mick Bates and Paul Reaney were recruited and there was optimism that City could make a successful promotion challenge. By the beginning of November City were fourth from bottom and it was clear that progress was not being made. Napier resigned and was replaced by George Mulhall. Despite five wins in succession (including an away victory at leaders Barnsley) during November and December City remained in a mid-table position for the rest of the season and finished 15th. One of the players introduced by Mulhall in the second half of the season was Peter Jackson. In this photograph Terry Dolan and Mick Wood are seen in action against Newport during the 1-3 defeat in September, 1978.

Right: Bobby Campbell established himself as a big hero at Valley Parade and was leading scorer during his first three full seasons. In December, 1983 he broke Frank O'Rourke's 69 year record as City's leading aggregate scorer. Campbell made a total of 319 League and Cup appearances for City and scored 143 goals between 1979 and 1986. In 1982 Campbell won two full caps for Northern Ireland and later became the first Bradford City player to be selected for a World Cup team squad.

R. Handley

Above: During the summer of 1980 there was again optimism that City would be one of the leading clubs in the division. Billy Ingham joined the club from Burnley in August, 1980 for a then record £30,000. However the 1980/81 season was one of disappointment with City finishing 14th and average League gates falling to a record low of 2,858. The last two games at Valley Parade were both watched by crowds of under two thousand including a record low of 1,249 for the game with Hereford. The highlight of that season was the 1-0 defeat of reigning League Champions Liverpool at Valley Parade in the first leg of the Second Round of the League Cup. Bobby Campbell was the man who scored City's goal but in the second leg it was Liverpool who emerged victorious with a 4-0 win. Les Chapman (no.11) and Bobby Campbell are closely marked by Thompson, Neal and Case of Liverpool at Anfield.

Right: The team that started the 1981/82 season comprised the players which Roy McFarland inherited as player-manager. The big difference was former England international Roy McFarland himself who played at the heart of the City defence. Joe Cooke returned to the club in

January, 1982 and was joined by Mark Lester also from Exeter the following month. Nine successive wins during September and October equalled the record set in 1953/54 and City suffered only two defeats in their last 25 games to secure promotion as runners-up. During the 1981/82 season they were defeated only five times away from home and they won 12 away games. The team was very stable with Ces Podd, Gary Watson, Barry Gallagher, Bobby Campbell and David McNiven (main picture, right) each making forty or more League appearances. City also enjoyed glory in the Football League Cup, drawing 1-1 at UEFA Cup holders and First Division runners-up Ipswich Town and only being beaten in extra time in the replay at Valley Parade. David McNiven formed a 'little and large' partnership with Bobby Campbell and scored 43 goals between them during 1981/82. In May, 1982 'Daisy' scored all four goals in the 4-1 defeat of Crewe.

Bradford City 1981/82 from left to right, rear: Podd, Hebditch, Campbell, Hanson and Jackson. Middle row: Jones (coach), Chippendale, Watson, Thompson, Ramsbottom, Smith, Wood, Watson, McCall and Edwards (Physio). Front: Chapman, Black, McNiven, Ingram, McFarland, Ellis, Staniforth and Gallagher.

Above: Stuart McCall played 238 League games for City between 1982 and 1988 in his first spell with the club and was made captain in November, 1986 at the age of 22.

Left: City versus Halifax Town in West Riding Cup tie in August, 1982. Peter Jackson challenges for the ball watched by Joe Cooke and Dave Staniforth (recently signed by Halifax from City).

At the end of October, 1982 City supporters could derive a certain amount of satisfaction from the fact that their team had established a mid-table position in Division Three and seemed strong enough to consolidate at this level. Three new faces had made their debuts for the club: Terry Gray, Ian Mellor and 18 year old Stuart McCall (left) deputising for Ces Podd at right back. The highpoint of the season was undoubtedly the League Cup tie with Manchester United at Valley Parade on 10 November in which Roy McFarland gave a tremendous performance to deny the visitors from scoring. The same evening there were rumours of McFarland's imminent return to Derby which indeed happened a fortnight later, days before the replay at Old Trafford. Stuart McCall was drafted into the team and although Bobby Campbell got on the scoresheet City were well beaten 1-4. The loss of McFarland was devastating and City's League form took an inevitable turn for the worse. Trevor Cherry and Terry Yorath were recruited in December but it was not until February that the club secured a win. During the second half of the season Cherry introduced six members of the team that was successful in winning the Northern Intermediate League Cup for the first time in the club's history. City finished a creditable 12th but few supporters were aware of the financial difficulties at Valley Parade which led to the end of the Martin era and a summer of trauma.

Chapter Five

Transformation 1983 - Present

The formal insolvency proceedings that commenced in June, 1983 were something of a shock to the Bradford public and there was also surprise at the seriousness of the club's financial position. Former chairman Stafford Heginbotham and Jack Tordoff led a rescue package but Bradford City's fight for survival was won as late as 6 August, 1983. Supporters pledged over £50,000 including one £10,000 anonymous donation. Twenty year olds Chris Withe (from Newcastle) and Garry Haire (from Whitley Bay) were signed by Cherry during the 1983 close season and they joined an already young squad. Perhaps the most significant change however was the sale of Bobby Campbell to Derby which was unavoidable given the financial circumstances. John Hawley was recruited as his replacement in August, 1983. The trauma and uncertainty of the summer meant that Cherry and Yorath had little time to prepare for their first full season at Valley Parade. City won once in their first 18 League and Cup games and struggled at the foot of Division Three with relegation looking almost inevitable. The turning point came in late November when Campbell returned from Derby and immediately formed a productive partnership with Hawley who had made an unimpressive start to the season. Hawley scored 20 goals in his last 31 games to be the leading scorer in 1983/84 with 23 goals from 45 League and Cup games. The team's record for the last 31

games of the season was promotion form with 19 wins and only six defeats. This included a record ten successive wins mid-way through the season as City lifted themselves from the bottom of the division. The team finished in seventh position and if they had not dropped 13 points out of the last 18 available it is arguable that they would have challenged for promotion. As a reflection of the progress made at Valley Parade during the 1983/84 season the reserve team finished as Champions of the Second Division of the Central League. Bobby Campbell is pictured celebrating one of his nine League goals in 1983/84.

More change has occurred at Valley Parade in the last two decades than since the turn of the century. Key defining moments which set about the transformation of the club were the appointment of Roy McFarland in May, 1981 and the fire disaster of May, 1985. However the insolvency of 1983 was probably a bigger turning point in Bradford City's history. It marked the end of the Martin era of financial mismanagement and fantastic schemes (most notably the Garside plan for the redevelopment of Valley Parade in 1980). Apart from the birth of a new company, BCAFC (1983) Ltd, those associated with the club at the time will testify to the great spirit which emerged both on the field and on the terraces during the 1983/84 season. The spirit sustained a new momentum delivering the so-called era of 'Bantam Progressivism', seven seasons of successive improvement in League standing between 1981-88.

Above: With limited money available Cherry was restricted to signing only two players during the summer of 1984 although both would prove to be influential during the 1984/85 season. Central defender Dave Evans came from Halifax and winger John Hendrie from Coventry. City made a slow start to the season and won three and lost three of their first seven League games but their form picked up from the beginning of October and a month later they were top of Division Three - a position they never lost. The team was very much similar to the previous season albeit with Evans taking Cherry's place in the centre of defence and Hendrie taking over from Garry Haire. Greg Abbott played in midfield, displacing Terry Gray, and then as right-back following the signing of midfielder Martin Singleton from Coventry in December. Don Goodman

emerged into the team partnering Bobby Campbell for 23 games during the middle of the season. Terry Yorath made one full appearance in September and announced his retirement shortly afterwards. Nine players made more than 40 League appearances and this brought a high degree of consistency. The team was also young and to all intents and purposes grew in maturity and strength as the season progressed.

Bradford City August, 1984. From left to right, back row: Mark Fletcher, Dave Evans, Chris Withe, Bobby Campbell, Eric McManus, Mel Gwinnett, John Hawley, Peter Jackson, Tony Clegg, Don Goodman, Micky Holmes and Brian Edwards (Physio). Middle: Terry Gray, John Hendrie, Gary Haire, Trevor Cherry, Terry Yorath, Stuart McCall, Mark Ellis, Greg Abbott and Micky Holmes. Front: Nigel Beaumont, Shayne Beeby, Phillip Kitching, John Reape, Trevor Nevinson, Gary Hodgsen, Andrew Walsh, Carl Hudson and Andy Laurence.

Left: In October, 1984 the award-winning Bradford City fanzine 'The City Gent' was born. It was one of the first of its kind in England and is now the oldest surviving independent supporters' publication still in circulation.

There were numerous performances that season which are worthy of mention, each characterised by the team's never-say-die spirit. The 7-2 thrashing of Tow Law Town in the First Round of the FA Cup was City's biggest win since the 6-0 defeat of Crewe in April, 1979 and memorable for substitute Don Goodman's quick hat-trick. The 1-2 defeat at Telford in the Third Round was the surprise of the season and the first time in 20 years that City had lost to non-League opposition. The injury to Eric McManus at Hull brought an element of drama when he was replaced in goal by Tony Clegg but City still beat their promotion rivals 2-0. McManus was briefly replaced by David Harvey who kept goal on the day City suffered the biggest defeat of the season, 0-4 at Millwall. Harvey's last game for City was the 5-4 victory over Brentford at Valley Parade in March which was certainly not for the faint hearted. Promotion was secured at Cambridge with a 4-0 victory but there were successive defeats at

Bournemouth (1-4) and at home to Reading (2-5) before the championship was clinched with a 2-0 win at Bolton in which Trevor Cherry played. In the picture below the victorious City team are seen celebrating at Bolton. City had been promoted in style with a club record 13 away wins and a record total of 28 wins. Four members of the City team that won the Northern Intermediate League Cup in 1982/83 played during the 1984/85 season, a tribute to the youth development programme at Valley Parade that had been launched by Roy McFarland.

SOCCER SHIELDS

BRADFORD CITY
No. 26

P. Suthers

This page: The last game of that successful season was supposed to be a day of celebration to mark the return of Bradford City to Division Two after 48 years in the lower divisions. Instead 11 May, 1985 is remembered for the tragic loss of 56 lives and the fire which destroyed the antiquated main stand on South Parade. Pictured with the Third Division trophy on that day from left to right: Chris Withe, John Hawley (part concealed), Don Goodman, Martin Singleton, Stuart McCall, Greg Abbott, Dave Evans, Peter Jackson (with trophy), Tony Clegg, John Hendrie, David Mossman, Bobby Campbell and Eric McManus.

Facing page: City's first season back in Division Two was always going to be difficult given that the club was effectively homeless and that home fixtures had to be played at Leeds (four games), Huddersfield (six) and Odsal Stadium, Bradford (eleven). For quite a long time there was uncertainty about where City would find a permanent home and thus it was something of an achievement that they finished 13th. The changes to the championship side were subtle with Eric McManus replaced by Peter Litchfield, Aidey Thorpe (signed from non-League Heanor) replacing John Hawley and Arthur Graham from Leeds taking the place of Mark Ellis. Trevor Cherry had retired and Don Goodman was restricted to only 19 appearances. Gavin Oliver was signed from Sheffield Wednesday in November, 1985 to play at right-back and made an immediate impact. A problem for the team was goals and three players ended the season as joint-top scorers with ten apiece, Greg Abbott, John Hendrie and Bobby Campbell. Campbell (pictured right in action with Stuart McCall against Huddersfield at Leeds Road) had found the transition to Division Two difficult having scored 23 goals in 46 League appearances the previous season. In September, 1986 he was sold to Wigan and replaced by Mark Leonard who was signed from Stockport for a then record £40,000. Ian Ormondroyd made his debut for City during the 1985/86 season making eight full appearances and four as substitute with three goals to his credit. Dave Evans is seen in action (right) during City's first League game at Odsal against Crystal Palace in November, 1985 which was won 1-0.

Above and right: Bradford City had to play a further ten home League fixtures at Odsal before moving back to Valley Parade for the game with Derby on Boxing Day, 1986. Of those games they managed to win only three, including a 2-0 victory over Leeds which was marred by their followers setting fire to a chip van in a pathetic attempt to have the game abandoned. The best games at Odsal were in the League Cup with wins over Newcastle and Portsmouth although the 0-5 defeat by Nottingham Forest was the exception. Peter Jackson was sold to Newcastle in October for a then record £250,000 (which the club could not afford to refuse) but this upset the composition of the defence. City's away form was unable to compensate for lost home points and by the turn of 1986 the club was in a relegation position with four successive defeats in December, including a 0-1 defeat to sour the homecoming. At least there had been some cheer when City had played an England XI to celebrate the opening of the new Valley Parade. Trevor Cherry was sacked in controversial circumstances in January, 1987 and Terry Dolan took charge of the team, initially as caretaker with Terry Yorath having already left to manage Swansea in 1986. Dolan's first game was the FA Cup Third Round replay against Division Two leaders Oldham which City won 5-1. In the Third Round

City played Everton at Valley Parade and despite losing 0-1 the team's performance did much to raise confidence. There was a relative improvement in League form but Dolan introduced three new players who made the difference to the team and eventually lifted it from the bottom four to tenth place. Former Manchester United reserve Karl Goddard (above) came into the team at left-back in January (replacing Robbie Savage who had previously displaced Chris Withe) and £70,000 record signing Brian Mitchell replaced Greg Abbott at right-back in February. Don Goodman was sold to West Brom in March and his place was taken by Abbott. The final piece in Dolan's jigsaw was Ron Futcher (top left) who was signed from Oldham in March and whose arrival inspired a run of seven wins and two draws out of the ten remaining League games.

A visit by the Prime Minister to Valley Parade in February, 1987.

Top: The 1987/88 season began with City winning the West Riding Cup for the fourth time in succession. During the close season goalkeeper Paul Tomlinson was signed from Sheffield United and defender Lee Sinnott was a £130,000 record signing from Watford. During the first 20 games of the season City won 13 and drew four to stay top of Division Two for ten weeks until the end of November when they were beaten 2-4 at home by Aston Villa. There was an indifferent run of form during December, and over the new year, by which time they had dropped to seventh. Mick Kennedy was signed from Portsmouth in January for a club record £250,000. He helped to strengthen the team who won eight and drew five of the next 14 games from the beginning of February to the end of April to climb to second position . City's penultimate game was at Aston Villa who were three points behind but with a better goal difference. Had City won they would have been promoted but in the event they were beaten 0-1. On the last day of the season they entertained Ipswich at Valley Parade knowing that they would secure promotion only if they won and both Middlesbrough and Aston Villa failed to do so. John Hendrie was forced to miss the game as a result of suspension and this would be the only League game he missed in four seasons at Valley Parade. Greg Abbott scored the first goal but Ipswich went into a 3-1 lead and eventually won 3-2 despite the fightback inspired by Stuart McCall. Lee Sinnott is seen in action during the Ipswich game (above). Ironically the other results had been in City's favour with Boro losing and Villa drawing to go up behind Millwall as runners-up. City finished fourth and played Middlesbrough in the play-offs. Despite a 2-1 win in the first leg at Valley Parade they lost 0-2 at Ayresome Park. The crucial factor in the play-offs had been full-back Brian Mitchell's absence arising from injury in the Ipswich game.

In subsequent years there has been much debate about whether the directors failed to provide sufficient funds for team strengthening but the evidence would suggest that it was not necessarily so black and white. It is true that City's small squad was severely stretched but promotion was lost as a result of critical home defeats and below par form on big occasions. The team had also been successful in cup competitions, reaching the Fifth Round of the League Cup (for only the second time in the club's history) and the Fifth Round of the FA Cup. Both campaigns undoubtedly added to the pressure and strains of the promotion challenge.

After finishing fourth in Division Two in 1988 City suffered four seasons of successive decline in League position with relegation in 1990 and their lowest position since promotion from Division Four in 1982 when they finished 16th in Division Three in 1992. Stuart McCall (left) and John Hendrie (facing page) had been sold during the summer of 1988 to Everton and Newcastle respectively, with City receiving a record fee of £850,000 for McCall. Ian Banks and Ian Thomas were recruited as replacements and in October, 1988 Peter Jackson returned as a record £290,000 signing. Although City briefly managed a position near the top of the division at the start of the season by March they were in a relegation place. Terry Dolan was replaced as manager in February, 1989 by Terry Yorath and the team eventually finished 14th. City's last two seasons in Division Two were characterised by a high degree of player turnover and very little stability. There were some questionable transfers which had more of a negative impact on club finances than a positive impact on

In 1988/89 City reached the Fifth Round of the League Cup for the second season in succession and the highlight was the 3-1 defeat of First Division Everton (for whom Stuart McCall was playing) at Valley Parade in the Fourth Round in December, 1988. Despite a home tie in the next round against a lower division club, City were beaten 0-1 by Bristol City. The League Cup defeat came less than a fortnight after City had beaten Spurs 1-0 at Valley Parade in the Third Round of the FA Cup. The scorer of City's goal (a penalty) was Brian Mitchell who is pictured second from the left at the front. To his left is Greg Abbott and to his right Mick Kennedy and Paul Jewell. The back row features (from left) Paul Tomlinson, Ian Banks, Leigh Palin, Dave Evans, Mark Leonard, Lee Sinnott and Peter Jackson. Defeat at home to Hull in the next round cost Terry Dolan his job.

appearances) joining Halifax and Mark Ellis (218) retiring. In March, 1990 Yorath was replaced by John Docherty but he was unable to prevent relegation and his favoured tactics made him extremely unpopular with supporters.

Below: (both pictures): Back in Division Three there was a further change of manager with Frank Stapleton arriving as player-manager in December, 1991. However the period 1990 to 1994 was undistinguishable and at no time during those four seasons were City realistic promotion contenders. The nearest they came was in 1994 when they finished in seventh position, just outside the play-offs. Neither was there any cup glory with City beaten by lower division opposition for three seasons in succession. In 1992 City were knocked out of the League Cup in the First Round by Scarborough; in 1993/94 they were beaten in the First Round of the FA Cup by Chester and the following season by Scunthorpe. One change at Valley Parade in the early nineties

the team. These included the signings of Mark Aizlewood, Alan Davies, Tony Adcock and Ian McCall. Jimmy Quinn was a good signing in March, 1989 but supporters failed to understand his subsequent sale to West Ham the following December. Peter Jackson's return was less than successful and he went to Huddersfield in September, 1990 as the club sought to cut its payroll. Jackson played 58 games for City in his second spell at the club which brought a total of 336 League appearances going back to 1978; this made him one of only ten players to make more than 300 League appearances for City. Two other long-serving players left the club in 1990 with Dave Evans (who had made 223 League

was the building of the double-tier Holywell Ash Lane stand in 1991. The photograph below features the City squad at the start of the 1990/91 season which was John Docherty's first full season in charge with City finishing 8th.

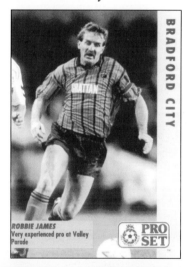

BRADFORD CITY

ROBBIE JAMES
Very experienced pro at Valley Parade

PRO SET

PAUL TOMLINSON

WAYNE JACOBS

GREG ABBOTT

BRADFORD CITY

BRIAN MITCHELL

BRADFORD CITY

EDDIE YOUDS

DES HAMILTON

Facing page: The turnover of players has been high throughout the nineties and it says much that Wayne Jacobs with 140 League appearances for City was the longest serving at the end of the 1997/98 season. The early part of the decade was more notable for the number of long-serving players who left the club such as Brian Mitchell (178 appearances) in January, 1992 and Greg Abbott (281) in August, 1991. However there have been a number of regulars this decade including Gavin Oliver (left) who made 313 League appearances for the Bantams between November, 1985 and January, 1995 and was awarded with a testimonial against Leeds in October, 1994. There was also Paul Tomlinson who completed 293 League appearances for City in 1995 and beat Jock Ewart's record for goalkeeping appearances which had stood for 67 years. Current manager Paul Jewell completed 269 appearances for City between 1988 and 1996 (of which 52 were as substitute) and Lee Duxbury played 272 games for City in two spells, 1989-94 and 1995-97. Lee Sinnott was transferred to Crystal Palace in August, 1991 and then returned to Valley Parade in December, 1993 before being transferred to Huddersfield a year later. In March, 1998 Sinnott returned again on loan from Oldham for a third spell and thereby completed 214 League appearances for Bradford City.

Below: City's average League attendances reached a peak of 12,906 in 1987/88 (the highest since 1949/50) but fell thereafter to average around half that level back in

the third division between 1990 and 1996. The club's finances deteriorated significantly and by 1994 it was once more heavily in debt. A new boardroom regime took over in February, 1994 from Dave Simpson who had presided over the doldrums of the early nineties. Geoffrey Richmond sacked Frank Stapleton and appointed Lennie Lawrence as manager with funds to finance new signings in an attempt to kick-start a recovery. John Taylor (a striker) was Lawrence's first signing for a record £300,000 from Bristol Rovers in August, 1994. City made a great start to the season with five wins and a draw in the first seven games but then lost their form and drifted downwards into a mid-table position to eventually finish 14th. Taylor was sold and it was long-serving Paul Jewell who ended the season as leading scorer with 14 goals.

Above: City were finally promoted from Division Two (the equivalent of the third division) in 1996 through the play-offs. The Bantams had been in a top-six position for a short period at the start of the season but there was a subsequent loss of form that led to the dismissal of Lennie Lawrence and the appointment of Chris Kamara as manager in November, 1995. Although City had beaten Nottingham Forest of the Premiership in the League Cup the team had been unable to play to its potential in the League itself. A late run including nine wins and a draw in the last 14 games lifted City from tenth to sixth and a place in the play-offs. In the first leg of the Play-Off Semi-Final City were beaten 0-2 at home to Blackpool. The second leg was more memorable as City managed an incredible 3-0 win with goals from Carl Shutt, Des Hamilton and Mark Stallard to go through to the Final on aggregate.

LEE POWER

JOHN TAYLOR

R. Halfpenny

Des Hamilton swept past three defenders and hammered the ball into the roof of the net. City were firmly in control but it wasn't until well into the second half that the lead was extended. Mark Stallard met Ian Ormondroyd's pass and scored City's second to secure victory and promotion to Division One (the second division) after an absence of six years. The victorious team were cheered by thousands of fans as they were taken in an open-top bus from Valley Parade to City Hall for a civic reception the next day. This was a special celebration which

Above: Victory at Blackpool earned Bradford City a trip to Wembley for the first time in the club's history. Thirty thousand Bradfordians travelled to London for the Division Two Play-Off Final against Notts County on 26 May, 1996 in what was probably the biggest ever exodus of football supporters from the city. The game was only seven minutes old when

had been denied eleven years before. The Wembley game generated interest in the club on a national and international scale from exiled Bradfordians. Many of those people took advantage of the internet to keep up to date with the news and thus the worldwide 'Internet Bantams' supporters network was established.

Below: A number of talented players were sold by the club during the nineties who have subsequently achieved fame and fortune elsewhere. These include Phil Babb in 1992, Graeme Tomlinson in 1995 (for whom a broken leg ended a career at Old Trafford), Mark Schwartzer and Des Hamilton in 1997 and Eddie Youds in 1998. Perhaps the most promising of them all was Dean Richards (pictured) who had made only 52 appearances for City before his transfer to Wolves for £1.85 million in June, 1995. Tomlinson and Hamilton had both played for the Bradford City team that progressed to the Semi-Finals of the FA Youth Cup in 1993/94. Ironically

one player who was selected for the Scotland World Cup Finals squad in 1998 had been released by the club ten months previously!

Bottom: City found the transition to Division One difficult and struggled for most of the 1996/97 season at the foot of the table. A record number of 42 players appeared for the club in League games with as many as ten nationalities represented (another record). The transfer record was twice broken first with the purchase of keeper Mark Schwartzer from Kaiserlautern for £350,000 and then Gordon Watson from Southampton for £550,000 (sadly he completed only two games before suffering a broken leg). Ultimately relegation was only avoided in the last game of the season with the 3-0 defeat of QPR. The signing of Chris Waddle by Chris Kamara in October, 1996 was an audacious move and although the former England international was 36 years old when he joined the club he had lost none of his skill. His finest moment for City in 28 League and Cup games came in the FA Cup Fourth Round tie at Everton in January, 1997 when he scored one of the greatest goals in FA Cup history. Waddle intercepted a poor clearance some 40 yards from goal and seeing that Neville Southall, the Everton keeper was off his line launched the ball goalward. The six thousand City fans rose in expectation (and it has to be said astonishment) as Southall raced back towards his goal: the ball went past Southall's outstretched arm and dropped into the net. City won the tie 3-2 and achieved their first victory at Goodison since April, 1909. The win earned City a place in the Fifth Round for the first time since 1988 but they were beaten by Sheffield Wednesday at Valley Parade.

On 27 March, 1997 Her Majesty the Queen was a visitor to Bradford as part of the city's centenary celebrations and she came to Valley Parade to officially open the Midland Road stand which had been completed three months earlier. In this photograph manager Chris Kamara is seen introducing the team.

The 1997/98 season was one of consolidation as City finished 13th, their highest position in the second division for ten years. Once more the transfer record was broken when John McGinlay joined from Bolton for £625,000. For a time there was talk of promotion as the team briefly topped the table but the season ended with a series of disappointing and inconsistent performances. Chris Kamara had already lost his job in January, 1998 and was later replaced by his former assistant, Paul Jewell. A highlight of the season was the winning of the Northern Intermediate League Cup for the first time since 1983.

It is already clear that the Richmond era will be recognised as a significant turning point in the history of Bradford City. Richmond is the first full-time chairman at Valley Parade and directs the club in accordance with strict financial principles without fear of making hard commercial decisions. His approach has brought a dramatic increase in gates and in 1997/98 the average League crowds were the highest for 68 years. The number of season ticket holders and the number of families attending games are both at record levels and by the end of the century Valley Parade will be an all-seater stadium for the first time in its history. Richmond has been successful in encouraging commercial sponsorship and generally improving the profitability and profile of the club (with Bradford City the most profitable football club in Yorkshire in 1997). His ambition is also relatively unprecedented and his impatience for success is reflected in the fact that he has sacked three managers in just four years. There has been a successive improvement in League position over the last three seasons and with the return of Stuart McCall to Valley Parade in June, 1998 as well as an unprecedented investment in new players including two one million pound signings in August, 1998, there is confidence that the momentum can be maintained. The next chapter in the story of Bradford City has only just begun!

THE AUTHOR

Thirty-five year old John Dewhirst was the co-founder of the award-winning CITY GENT in 1984 which was one of the first independent football supporters' publications in the UK and is now the oldest surviving. In 1988 he assisted with 'Of Boars and Bantams' by Don Gillan and in 1997 was co-author of 'Along the Midland Road', a history of Valley Parade, with Dave Pendleton. Earlier in 1998 he also helped to produce 'Paraders Past', a video featuring the oldest surviving film of Valley Parade and Bradford City in League action. John is a Financial Director of a Guiseley based firm, and married to Helen, a Bradford GP. He has three children, Harry, Sarah and Alison and lives in Shipley.

ACKNOWLEDGMENTS

The author would like to thank all the people who have assisted in various ways with this project in particular the following:

Dave Pendleton, Mick Jones, Peter Suthers, Chris Gilliver (Bradford City AFC), John Watmough, Richard Halfpenny, Dave Roper, Brian Mitchell, Alf Jeffries, Mary Burras, Malcolm Hartley, Kevin Tempest, Ken Teasdale, Don Gillan, David Fell, Keith Bruce, Peter Fieldhouse, David Burnet, Donald Boocock, Graham Hall, Julian Toothill, Kath Brodie, Tim Clapham, Ray Dawes, Barbara Jackson (Midland Bank), Ray Spiller (AFS), Maura McGolgan.

PRESENTATION COPIES OF CITY MEMORIES

Alf Jeffries, player 1935-37, **Ken Teasdale,** player 1943-45, **David Jackson,** player 1955-61, **Ian Cooper,** player 1965-76, **Bruce Bannister,** player 1965-71, **Bobby Ham,** player 1968-70 and 1973-75, **Ces Podd,** player 1970-84, **Bryan Edwards,** manager 1971-75, **Allan Gilliver,** player 1972-74 and 1979, **Terry Dolan,** player 1976-81 and manager 1987-89, **Bobby Campbell,** player 1980-83 and 1983-86, **Stuart McCall,** player 1982-88 and 1998 to date, **John Hendrie,** player 1984-88, **Gavin Oliver,** player 1985-95, **Brian Mitchell,** player 1987-92, **Lee Sinnott,** player 1987-91, 1993-94 and 1998, **Paul Jewell,** player 1988-96 and manager 1998 to date

PRE-PUBLICATION SUBSCRIBERS TO CITY MEMORIES

Harry Dewhirst	Dave Pendleton, The City Gent	Richard Halfpenny, The City Gent
Sarah Dewhirst	John Watmough, The City Gent	Gill Otto, The City Gent
Alison Dewhirst	Paul Wood	Paul Donnelly
Kevin Halligan	Andrew Ellis	Keith B. Crowther
Daniel Halligan	Peter Ellis	Michael Grayson
Conor Halligan	R.I. Hainsworth	Michael J.W. Barr
David Scally	Michael Jones	David C. Lovedale
Robert Vale	Robert M. Rishworth	Graham Robertson
Denis Vale	Philip D. Clarke	Tom Stableford
Paul R. Smith	Raymond Dawes	John Treleven
David J. Moore	James Lovedale	Alex. Paul Grace
Andrew D. Pickles	Geoffrey Moses	Richard Illingworth
Susan Gross	Geoff Flynn	Paul J. Firth
Lee Yarnold	Trond Otrebski Langfjaeran	Derek Pickles
The Bundesbantams	Gerrard Myers	Michael Pendleton
Brian Allinson	Algis Rekesius	Chris Marsh
D.B. Mitchell	Chris Armstrong	Carl Hardy Barber
Mick Skelton	Paul Cuthbertson	Melvyn Daisey
Colin Illingworth	Chris Hawkridge	Richard Stretton
Timothy Williamson	John Cook	Paul Martin Guest
Mark Williamson	Linda Cook	Keith Wildman
Aidan Fletcher	Anthony & Matthew Cook	Mark Hassall
Kieran Fletcher	Graham Rollinson	Leslie Gudgeon
Alan Biggins	Stephen Gant	Paul Hirst
Chris Morrison	Stephen Benson	The Wings of a Sparrow fanzine
David Fenton	Graham R. Coultous	Dave Welbourne
David Greenwood	Mr & Mrs Eric Lee	Darren Wilding
Iain Moore	Robert Hiley	Emma Wilding
Tony (Eric) Moore	Richard Sykes	Michael John Illingworth
Neil Holley-Williams	Phil Jenkins	Craig Wilding
Paula Holley-Williams	Adam Cobb	Philip Joyce
Oliver Holley-Williams	Ian Ridley	Chris Overend
Beverley Claire Frances Calam	Tim Barker	Stanley Wilkinson
Tony Watson	D.I. Storey	Ken Dorrington
Revd Nigel Mason	Assctn of Sports Historians	Deirdre Dorrington
James Roberts	Jonathan Kerry	Andrew Hebden
Peter Bell	Tony Johnson	Jack H. Atkinson
Leslie Bell	David J. Mitchell	Damian Stead
Betty Bell	P.H.E. Partovi	Philip Walker
Andrew Flett	Patrick Brady	Roger (Trotwood) Nowell
Neil Turner	B. Danylczuk	Michael Baker
Sharon Turner	Robert Edward Wainwright	Harry Baker
Sarah Turner	Stuart Loxton	Manny Dominguez
Chris Pollard	Jonathan Clough	Andy Waller

Daniel Greenwood	C.M. Breen	Joanne L. Clegg
Martin Greenwood	Graham Leng	John Foster
Jeffrey Spolnik	John Owen	Gavin Dimmock 30
Adam Spolnik	Rob Renold	Gareth Beardall
Maurice Thirkill	Robert A.R. Dimbleby	Gary Ormondroyd
Matthew J.M. Martindale	Barbara Jackson, Midland Bank	Charles Walter Turner
Jonathan Mortimer	P. Suthers	Peter Charles Turner
V.J. Waddington	Patrick John Swithinbank	Richard Hainsworth
Martin J. Davison	Robert Kelly Swithinbank	Danny Higson
Rob Hunt	Harrison Family	Nick Asquith
James Derek Willis	Antony Hudson	Bob Lilliman
David Jackson	Sue Wellings	Roger Wash
Ian Macleod	Phil Wellings	David M. Woods
Raymond James Allen	Stephen Connell	Richard Palmer
Keith Bruce	Christopher Hladowski	Stephen Abberton
Peter L. Holmes	Mark Rymer	Christopher Abberton
Arran Matthew Lodge	Tim Rymer	Jason Parker
Neil Walker	Darren Wayne Slingsby	David Fell
Andy Ward	Eric R. Toulmin	Chris Wilkinson
Malcolm Gardner	Chris Kay	Geoff Bruce
Madge West	J.V. Blamire	Daniel Lee Ward
Keith Hall	James Lunn	Karl South
John Brewis	Raymond Shaw	Paul A. Smith
Terry Dickinson	General Boyle	Keith Coburn
Chris Burgess	Benjamin Scott Cunliffe	Kieron Coburn
Robert Amato	Sophie Hope Cunliffe	Julie Poucher
G. David Burnet	Catherine O'Rourke McColgan	Barry Cropper
Gerland Bell	Graham Hall	Joseph Keenan
Dave Howker	John Harris	David Pease
Martin Walker	David Keats	David Hill
Paul Farndale	Moira & Frederick Furness	Gary Bennett
Steve Clarke (1958-1998)	Geoff Allman	David J. Benham
Tim Peake	Bob McPherson	S.J. Brown
T.G.D. Capstick	David Knott	Jonothan Stringer
John A.W. Clough	Robin Pointon	James C.B. Thomas
Andrew Bambrough	John Booth	Paul J.E. Jennings
D.G. Ratcliffe	Phil Artus	James A. McLaren
Iain Morris	Brian Tewkesbury	Paul G. Collinge
M.J. Kelly	Brian David Dimmock	Edward Alan Oliver
J. Kelly	Stan Eibin	Michael Levycky
T. Kelly	Jonathan Carr	Jonathan Moore
Jacob Clark Inman	Daniel Brodie	Simon Ashdown

Bradford City, 1921/22

Mark Ashdown	Matthew J. Kermode	Nigel Newton
Ben Ashdown	Malc Hartley	Gemma Newton
Sam Ashdown	Jack Fothergill	Michael Sansom
Josie Ashdown	Colin Parker	Neal Ackroyd
Tom Ashdown	Mike Scott	Martin Ackroyd
Janine Emsley	Gregory Markham	Gareth Ackroyd
Scott Emsley	John Loxam	Kenneth W. Lodge
Alan Maude	Molly Jewitt	Michael Bowen
Andrew Ives	Samuel Jewitt	Michael Firth
Stuart Williamson	Alan Wood	Stuart F. Lupton
Brian Hainsworth	Alexandra Webster	Paul Anthony Gallagher
Peter Chadwick	Hannah Webster	Jack Tyne
Richard Holden	Sarah Webster	Paul Simon Callaghan
John Ringrose	Paul L. Thompson	Malcolm Watson
Mikael Eklof	Mark Thorp	Oliver Watson
Guy Thornton	Kenneth Waddington	Marcus Crabbe
Peter Waller	Stephen Gant	Charles Philip Clark
The Frankfurt Bundesbantam	Kenneth D. Fryer	Martin Bailey
Ray Adlam (Gloucester)	Maurice Docwra	Mick Gibson
Michael Callahan	Martin Kemp	Michael Costello
Michael George Handley	Gerard Baines	Trevor Hynd
Graham Robinson	Matthew Toulmin	David M. Booth
David Robertshaw	Steven Ogden	Paul Hazon
Anthony Stephen Firth	Tony Williamson	Ian Purdham
G.J. Pearson	Tom Booth	Neil Ideson
Philip John Allen	John Charles Smith	Gregory Troy
Malcolm Collins	Nicholas O'Melia	Mark Williams
Geoff Crossley	Clifford Walsh	George Kowalczyk
S.M. Durrant	Sandra Walsh	Stuart Wright
Simon Durrant	Phillip Richard Nelson	Rick Green
Chris Durrant	Matthew John Townsend	Karen Green
Holly Durrant	Miles Horsley	Alwyn Haggis
Tony Jagger	Dean Lamb	Joseph Donlon
Robert Goodall	Michael Lamb	Brian Robinson
Stephen Goodall	Leslie Briggs	Bert Brear
Sean O'Grady	David Fairclough	James Womack
David Wilkins	Kevin Collier	Mark Darren Crabtree
Richard Jones	Margaret Rose Brown	John Bussey
Euan Watson	Jack Williams	Matthew Woollias
Peter Clay	Tracey Duffield	Susan Sayles
Michael Kennedy	John Joyce	Karen Sayles
Paul Cook	John Musgrave	Stephen T. Wade

CITY MEMORIES

Richard Gudgeon
Andrew May
Robert Gary Ingham
David J. Moore
Richard C. Thackray
Andrew N.J. Newby
Dave Thompson
Richard A. Johnston
Adam Bell
Andrew Franks
Darran Stephen Slator
Stanley Yeadon
Steve Farrell
Robert Kingsley Cross
C.A. Jackson
H. Glover
Peter Edward Clay
Anthony Smith
Michael Stewart Driver
Chris Menaul
Ian Swithenbank
Paul Martyn Stapleton
Keith Steven Lee
David J. Clarkson
Matthew Elener
Michael A. Birdsall
Ian Patrick Kelly
Ian Fairhurst
Kim Stephanie King
James Fry
Willi Rabe
John B. Hodgson
Ralph Scott
John A. Stokes
Norman Blissitt
Stephen Michael Conroy
Michael Parrish
Steven Lightowler
Barry William Town
Paul Andrew Town
Chris Bailey
Richard Bailey
Michael Den Haz Doyle
Paul Wayne Hird
Christine Moore
Matthew Mears
Alex Batchelor
Chris Jackson
John Edwards
Jim Beveridge
Peter Davies
David Burrows
Les Gunde
David Perry
Peter Jenner
Chris Mansell

Henry Otford
Alan Ainsley
Richard Taylor
Jon Middlebrook
J.J. Burnel
Greg Hendon
Craig Newcastle
Martin Hapton
Andy Stevenson
Jackie Gamble
Craig Whiteley
Ben Richards
Julian Bentham
Michael Porter
Jane Smith
Richard Southam
Gareth Mountleigh
Dave Sampson
Simon Thompson
Julie Thompson
Rod Thompson
Dirk Schwinger
Mike Winterton
James Morrison
Vicky White
Harry Grant
Sydney Hayes
David Russell
Alison Ford
Ian Wetherby
Leslie Wetherby
Mary Murdoe
Ann Whitehead
Malcolm Whitehead
Martin Ramsden
James Worsman
Chris Welbourne
Rodney Sykes
Peter Dolby
Stephen Hanson
Steve Abbott
Alistair J. Petty
Colin & Margaret Richardson
Daniel Lee Mottram
John Kendall
Kirk Lacy
Vicky Wallace
Sue Wellings
Paul Elkins
Ian Hollings
Christopher Ingleby
Brian Knapton
David A. Overton
Geoff Mullinder
Marko Kristovic
Andrea Boyes

Nicolas Fedynyszyn
Robin C. Brockett
Paul Hughes
Jonathan Forrest
Michael Welch
Douglas Powell
Anthony Hodges
Andrew Rishworth
Ronnie Hill
John Northcutt

Andrew Marshall
Emma Parkinson
Matthew Parkinson
Harry Blott
Richard Bland
Clifford Dawson
Peter Sayer
Trevor Thomas
Dave Baker
Willy Webb
Michelle Boocock
Mark Boocock
Susan Boocock
Allan Nutton
A. Hillier
Bernadette O'Neill
Andrew Padgett
Darren Feather
Sarah Tomlinson
Matthew Shackleton
Janet Rawnsley
Irene Bulman
Eddie Neville
Andy Carter
Nicky Lobodzinski
Andrew Lobodzinski
Stephen Kondri
Keith W. Mills
Catherine E. Lange
Richard Lange
Darren Hird
Nick Taylor, The Fountain
Darren J. Richards
Christian D. Richards
Kenneth Steward
Roger North
Michael Forrest
Julian Ostrowski
Isabel Ostrowski
Rev Malcolm G. Lorimer
Denis Sharkey
Richard Palmer
Simon James Lister
Andrew Pitts